CROSS STITCH
CASTLES &
COTTAGES

Jane Greenoff

A DAVID & CHARLES CRAFT BOOK

To my husband Bill, without whose love and support
this book could not have been started and to
my children, James and Louise, without whose patience
it could not have been finished

Photography by Dudley Moss and Di Lewis
Cover design stitched by Hanne Castelo

Text and illustrations © Jane Greenoff

British Library Cataloguing in Publication Data
Greenoff, Jane
  Cross stitch castles and cottages.
  1. Embroidery. Cross-stitch – Patterns
  I. Title
  746.44

  ISBN 0-7153-9342-1

Typeset by Typesetters (Birmingham) Ltd,
Smethwick, West Midlands
and printed in West Germany
by Mohndruck GmbH
for David & Charles Publishers plc
Brunel House   Newton Abbot   Devon

Distributed in the United States by
Sterling Publishing Co. Inc,
Park Avenue, New York, NY 10016

CONTENTS

FOREWORD

This book is aimed at anybody who has picked up a kit in a shop, seen that the design is not printed on the fabric and put it back again. It is aimed at beginners, experts and enthusiasts alike.

My addiction to cross stitch began by accident five years ago. I had given up nursing to have my son James and really looked forward to the future as a housewife and mother, but, after fifteen years of working in hospitals, the change took more adjustment than I had expected. After six months my husband's work moved us to the Cotswolds and from a modern house to a listed cottage more than three hundred years old. We began collecting old furniture and bric-a-brac to complement our new home and I developed what could only be described as a passion for old samplers. I seemed to be able to sense their existence in the corners of antique shops and I have certainly almost caused an accident screeching to a halt outside a shop with needlework in the window. Unfortunately, the objects of my passion were far too expensive for our already stretched budget so I had to think again.

About this time a neighbour showed me a piece of exquisite needlework. On examination, the fabric was quite devoid of transfer or printing so I was completely baffled. Then followed my first lesson in counted cross stitch. To say that I was hooked was no exaggeration!

After a fruitless search for a suitable sampler kit in the local shops, I planned my first sampler. Looking back it was quite dreadful, but I did enjoy those hours with graph paper and pens. From these humble beginnings I discovered that I had a talent for designing charts of buildings and village scenes and have developed a flourishing little business making needlework kits for the trade.

Cross stitch has brought me a great deal of pleasure and satisfaction – I hope this book will help to spread that enjoyment to a few more people.

INTRODUCTION

Embroidery is, by definition, a way of decorating and embellishing a piece of fabric or a garment, and it can be traced back thousands of years. One of the earliest surviving pieces of needlework is probably South American and dates back to AD200. This piece depicts animals, figures and mythological creatures and experts believe it may have been a record of patterns or stitches – one of the first 'examplers', or samplers as we have come to know them.

It is not known exactly when samplers became part of European tradition, although written evidence suggests their existence in the early part of the sixteenth century. At this time no printed patterns or books of needlework existed, so women would keep an 'exampler' as a memorandum of designs. (In medieval English the term 'exampler' denoted a model or pattern to be copied or imitated.) The earliest known sampler to be signed and dated was worked by Jane Bostocke in 1596 and is now in the Victoria and Albert Museum in London. The sampler was stitched on unbleached linen and Jane had used many stitches including cross, back, satin, ladder, buttonhole, plus bullion bars and french knots. Later designs, from about 1700 onward, are the more familiar shapes and styles with borders, alphabets and often a house, church or castle incorporated. As with the projects described in this book, the main stitch was cross stitch, supplemented by french knots, back stitch, four-sided stitch, tent stitch and several others.

Cross stitch was one of the many needlepoint stitches used by the Victorians in Berlin work cushions, chair-seat covers and pictures. These designs would often illustrate vases of flowers, bowls of fruit, scenes from nature, etc. At the same time, cross stitch continued to be the most popular stitch used for commemorative samplers of the day. In fact, it has never ceased to be popular and is today enjoying a strong increase in interest – in both traditional and experimental embroidery.

SEEKING INSPIRATION

There is a large number of excellent reference books available with good colour illustrations of samplers and other needlework (see Bibliography). Information can often be found in auction house catalogues, but you must be prepared just to browse, as antique embroidery can cost a small fortune! Embroiderers' guilds and sewing groups sometimes have antique collections for reference and will occasionally arrange trips to private collections.

Computer games and programs provide another, perhaps surprising, source of ideas. After all, computers and cross stitch both use designs based on squares!

Last, but not at all least, browsing through specialist needlework shops can give you all sorts of ideas, as can studying some of the cross stitch and embroidery magazines. Above all, you must learn to be aware of design ideas from the most unlikely and everyday objects. But beware, this hobby can become obsessive!

WHAT IS COUNTED CROSS STITCH?

Embroidery can be grouped into two main categories: free embroidery where the stitches are unrelated to the background weave of the fabric; and counted thread embroidery where the stitches are worked by counting the threads of the material. Counted needlework has enormous scope, because you the stitcher are in control. You are not dependent on the designer, kit manufacturer or even the author's ideas, as the fabric is clear of transfer, printing or any other form of distraction.

The design is transferred on to the fabric by positioning each stitch using the chart as the pattern and the threads of the fabric as a guide. It is the most personal sort of needlework where you are creating a true original every time – satisfying to keep or give to friends. A special gift, however small, because you made it.

The first chapter in this book describes the materials you will need and the second tells you how to begin sewing for yourself. At this point a novice can often be seen to panic; the crisp clean fabric can be so daunting to the uninitiated. The cry is heard, 'Oh, I need it printed on. It is so much easier!', but this is just not true. With some printed designs, if the printing is not very accurate, the stitches can appear out of position and the results can be disappointing. Once you have mastered counting you will never buy a printed design again.

Although this book is principally about cross stitch, which is usually worked in cotton threads on evenweave line, aida or hardanger, some of the designs are worked on canvas with wools to show the contrast between the two mediums. Once you have grasped the principles of working from charts you will be able to work the designs on anything.

Where stranded cotton reference numbers are mentioned in the book these refer to the Anchor (Bates) range of colours. These can be exchanged for DMC shades if preferred. Imperial measurements have been used when associated with the thread counts because many fabrics are supplied in Imperial sizes. Metric conversions for design sizes are included in each chapter.

CHAPTER 1
MATERIALS AND EQUIPMENT

FABRICS

For any form of counted needlework you will need an evenweave fabric. This simply means that the weft (horizontal threads) and the warp (vertical threads) are woven evenly to give the same number of threads in each direction. The designs are based on a square stitch so it is vital that the fabric has an evenweave (see Fig 1). Although it would be possible to count the threads on ordinary linen correctly, your stitches could become squashed and the design distorted.

Fabric choice is a matter of personal taste and knowing your own and your eyesight's limitation; stitchers often become discouraged and give up when the choice of fabric is the problem rather than the skill of the stitcher.

To start with, choose a fabric you can see without too many artificial aids; you can advance to finer, more delicate fabric when you have mastered the technique. When buying fabric check with the assistant to ensure you are on the right lines.

LINEN

Although a good quality evenweave linen is quite expensive, it is lovely to handle and lends itself to delicate cross stitch. When using linen the cross stitches are worked over two strands in each direction (see Fig 1).

AIDA AND HARDANGER

These cotton fabrics have been specially produced for counted needlework. The threads are woven in blocks rather than singly and a cross stitch is worked over a single block (see Fig 2).

The projects in this book have used other fabrics and materials as well as linen and aida, but these are ideal for perfecting your techniques. Remember, any of the designs in the book can be worked on any fabric so long as it is evenweave.

Fig 1 A cross stitch on
evenweave linen

Fig 2 A cross stitch on aida

THREADS

During the last decade the numbers of threads (both natural and synthetic) available for needlework have increased tenfold and it would be impossible to discuss them all here. A variety of materials have been used in the book and will be discussed later. The list that follows is just to whet your appetite.

STRANDED COTTON (Floss)

This is probably the most commonly used embroidery thread and is generally available in one form or another. Where a stranded cotton has been used in the models photographed, the shade numbers referred to are Anchor threads (Bates), although you can substitute other makes if desired.

Stranded cotton is made up of six strands of mercerised cotton (this gives the thread the familiar sheen and finish). The thread is usually split into the number of strands required as you stitch. Each design in the book will indicate how many strands to use, although you can always experiment with your own ideas.

Care and management of threads and materials will be dealt with in a separate section.

PERLE COTTON

A highly mercerised twisted non-divisible cotton thread, with a subtle gloss when stitched.

FLOWER THREAD

A soft un-mercerised cotton thread with a fine matt finish.

RAYON THREAD

Shiny man-made thread with a strong gloss and usually in vibrant colours. It can be very effective when a striking contrast is required.

DESIGNER SILKS

This comparatively new thread is a spun Chinese silk, which is dyed by hand, using acid dyes. The Designer Silks used in the book are space dyed and blended throughout the spectrum, so that the colour changes are subtle and the lustre of the silk is used in the design.

CREWEL WOOL

This soft two-ply wool is ideal for both tapestry and cross stitch, and is usually worked in two or more strands.

TAPESTRY WOOL

A non-divisible four-ply wool that is ideal for canvas work and other creative embroidery. It can be very useful when large amounts of canvas need to be covered.

CHOOSING THREADS

Choosing embroidery threads can be quite daunting, but there are a few ground rules to keep in mind.

Always have the fabric you intend to use as a background with you when choosing threads, as it will affect your choice of colours. When in the shop, move to the daylight, or where available use a daylight box (a special light that does not affect the colour shades).

Do not be alarmed by the vast ranges of coloured thread to choose from. Frequently, similar shades blended together can be most effective. As you examine the charts in the book you will notice that the colours are often just a shade apart to add texture without too much contrast.

After working a few designs you will find it easier to choose colours and make fewer mistakes so do not worry about early mishaps.

CARING FOR THREADS

If you can remember returning to an old piece of needlework and finding a tangled mass of muddled colours this section is for you!

One of the most successful ways of keeping your threads in some sort of order whilst stitching is to use an organiser. You can buy these, but just as easily you can make your own. You will need stiff card with punched holes

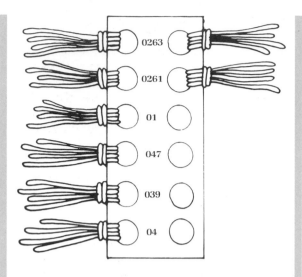

Fig 3 A thread organiser

down each side (see Fig 3). If you unwind a skein of stranded cotton and cut this into manageable lengths, they can be threaded through the holes and labelled with their shade number (see Fig 3.

It is quite easy to remove one length of thread without disturbing all the rest. To divide the cotton, just split the number of threads you need and gradually pull apart. Do not jerk the threads because they tend to tangle. If you return the spare colours to the vacant hole opposite the shade number it will prevent muddle later.

THE CHARTS

A needlework chart may be a series of symbols or coloured squares on graph paper (see p21). The principle is the same for either type.

Each square, both occupied and un-occupied, represents two threads of linen or one block of aida. Each occupied square (ie one that contains a symbol or colour) equals one stitch. At this stage each stitch is presumed to be a completed cross stitch, as other techniques will be explained later in the book.

The colours on the charts are as close as possible to the thread used, but this is always limited to the available colouring materials and to the accuracy of colour reproduction. For this reason, some of the charts in the book will have a complete key to the threads used, and others will offer a guide only and will suggest shades and types of threads most suitable. You can, of course, use alternatives either from preference or because of the difficulty finding a particular product.

Charts using symbols with a colour code may look complicated, but with practice you will be able to visualise the finished result without the use of coloured crayons. As you become more expert you may wish to add colours to, or subtract colours from, your designs and may even add new materials to enhance your work.

The designing of charts using both colour and symbols will be explained later in the book.

HOW TO CALCULATE DESIGN SIZE

First, look at the chart and count the stitches in each direction, ie the number of squares on the chart that are coloured or are occupied by a symbol. Test yourself by counting the squares on one of the charts in the chapter 'First Projects' and comparing the number with the given stitch count. Here's an example: 168 stitches (horizontal) × 140 stitches (vertical).

Next, check your chosen fabric to calculate how much you will need. You will need to know its thread count to estimate the completed dimensions: place a ruler on top of your fabric and, using a needle, count the number of threads or blocks to the inch. A cross stitch is worked over two threads in each direction when using linen and one block if using aida. Therefore, if the linen has 28 threads to the inch, there will be 14 stitches to the inch and so on. Using our stitch count example of 168 stitches × 140 stitches, the calculation is as follows:

168 @ 14 stitches to the inch = 12in
(horizontal finished size)
140 @ 14 stitches to the inch = 10in
(vertical finished size)

When the thread count of the fabric changes so will the finished size of the design. The following table shows how much the finished size of our example would vary with different fabrics.

Fabric/Thread count (per inch)	Stitch count (per inch)	Finished size
Linen/28 threads	14	12×10in
Linen/30 threads	15	11¼×8in
Aida/14 [blocks]	14	12×10in
Aida/18 [blocks]	18	9⅓×7¾in

The crucial factor with any counted needlework is the number of stitches in the design; this and the thread count of the fabric will determine the size of the completed project. Remember, if you use a different fabric from the one shown in your chosen project, the finished size will be different.

HOW MUCH FABRIC WILL YOU NEED?

Once you have your finished design size, it is time to decide how much fabric to buy. It is vital to add on a reasonable border for stretching and framing; about 3in (7.5cm) all the way round is a good guideline, although less could be appropriate for a very small design.

Some shops will sell linen and aida in pieces, but it is more common to buy the length you require from a roll which involves buying the full width of the fabric as well. This will enable you to work a number of projects or possibly share with a friend.

Once purchased, keep the fabric wrapped and safe from coffee, marmalade and the cat!

WASHING NEEDLEWORK

The best solution here is not to have to wash a project at all. It is not an ideal world, however, and accidents happen even in the best circles. The threads used in needlework are not always colour fast and so great care must be taken when attempting to wash even a small part of a project. Stranded cottons can usually be relied on not to run, as can most of the silk threads on the market, but only if you follow the manufacturer's instructions.

A good rule of thumb is to use lukewarm water and soap flakes, although the European Silk Commission recommend Tenestar, which contains no bleach.

TO FRAME OR NOT TO FRAME

Whether or not to use a frame is very much a personal choice, although some designs are easier to manage on some form of frame or hoop.

HOOPS

Various sizes of hoops are available and these can be very helpful when stitching a small design. Only use a hoop if the whole design will fit inside, because moving the hoop can distort the fabric and your carefully sewn stitches!

In later chapters where silk painting is included, a hoop must be used to keep the fabric taut whilst tinting.

Some shops now stock hoops that can be used to frame the project after being used to hold the fabric during stitching. These can be most attractive and are generally inexpensive (see p 33).

FRAMES

Rectangular frames also come in a variety of sizes and styles, some with floor or table stands to keep both hands free. The needlework is stitched to the webbing along the width of the frame, and the excess fabric is held on the rollers at the top and bottom (see Fig 4).

Upholstered frames can be made for the enthusiast as the needlework is then just pinned to the wadding and can be removed easily.

FRAMELESS STITCHING

If you prefer to work without a frame you may find that you work faster, but care must be taken to keep your tension even and neither too tight nor too slack.

Later in the book projects are described that need special techniques for working with silk gauze; these are explained in the relevant chapter.

SCISSORS

You will need a sharp pair of dressmaking scissors for cutting your fabric. When cutting linen or aida it is important to follow the line of threads to make sure you have a straight edge. To check that the fabric is straight, pull out a thread at the edge and then trim to match if necessary.

A small pair of pointed embroidery scissors is an essential accessory so that the stitcher may trim the ends of threads and can easily unpick the work when all else fails.

A scissor keeper (like a weighted pin cushion) tied to the scissors will make them easier to find (unless you prefer to wear them around your neck).

NEEDLES

With all counted needlework you will need ball point or blunt tapestry needles, which will need to vary in size depending on the fabric and the thread in use. Choosing a needle will depend on your preference and, more important still, the fabric you are using. The needle should slip through the fabric without enlarging the hole, but should not fall through without a little pressure.

Whilst considering needles in general, avoid leaving the needle in the fabric when you put it away as it can leave marks and may even rust. On some designs, to save chopping and changing every few stitches, you may find it helpful to use a number of needles with different colours threaded, especially whilst stitching a coloured border (see Fig 23, p 53).

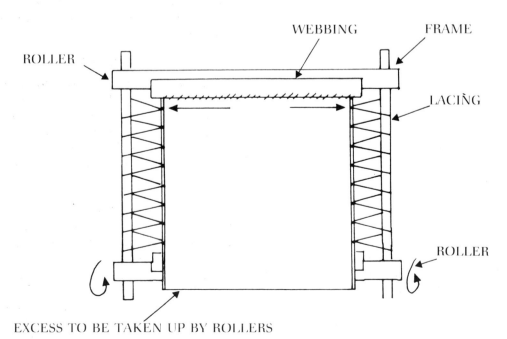

Fig 4 A needlework frame

CHAPTER 2
CROSS STITCH EXPLAINED

A cross stitch is formed by working two crossing arms on the fabric (see Fig 1). It can be worked in one of two ways. A completed stitch can be worked or a number of half stitches can be sewn to be completed on the return journey (see Fig 5). Both methods have their good

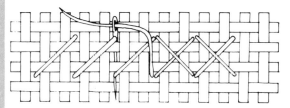

Fig 5 Cross stitch worked in two journeys

and bad points, and you should suit yourself and, of course, the design you arc working.

The essential ingredient of each cross stitch is that each top stitch goes in the same direction.

Methods of Starting

As in all forms of needlework, using a knot to anchor the first stitch is frowned upon, unless you plan to cut it off once the work is started (see Fig 6). This is not just the puristic view. A knot causes an unsightly mass at the back of your work, can pull through to the right side when the work is stretched, and gets in the way of later work.

KNOT ON THE RIGHT SIDE

After threading your needle, and knotting the end, pierce the fabric on the right side away from your intended stitch. Bring the needle up through the fabric where you intend to start your first cross, and work three or four stitches towards the knot, thus anchoring the thread. Push the needle to the

back of the work and, checking that the thread is anchored, snip off the excess thread and the knot from the front.

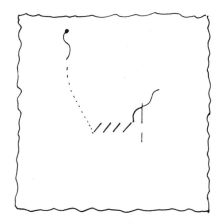

Fig 6 A knot on the right side

Avoid using this method with very dark colours, particularly black, as they can leave small marks which take time to remove. (A small clean toothbrush is very useful for removing unwanted whiskers.)

KNOT ON THE WRONG SIDE

Bring the needle up where you intend to start, feeling the knot with the other hand and leaving about an inch of thread. Work a few stitches then return to the wrong side, anchor the thread and snip off the extra thread and the knot.

KNOTLESS LOOP START

This method can be very useful with stranded cotton, but does not work unless you intend to stitch with two strands. Cut the stranded cotton to roughly twice the length you would usually sew with, and carefully separate just one strand. Double this thread and thread your needle pushing the two cut edges through the eye. Pierce your fabric

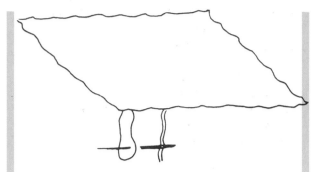

Fig 7 Knotless loop start

from the wrong side where you intend to start your first stitch, leaving the looped end at the rear of the work (see Fig 7). Return your needle to the wrong side after forming a half cross stitch and pass the needle through the waiting loop. Thus the stitch is anchored and the work can continue.

THE COMPLETED STITCH

For this example the stitch is worked on linen, over two strands of the fabric with two strands of stranded cotton.

Bring the needle up through the wrong side at the bottom left and cross two threads and insert at top right. To do this either count two up and two along or vice versa. Push the needle through and bring up at the bottom right hand corner, ready to complete the cross stitch (see Fig 1). The thread will cross your first stitch and your first cross stitch will be completed.

To work the adjacent cross, bring the needle up at the bottom right hand corner of the first stitch, thus the stitches share points on entry and exit.

PART COMPLETED STITCHES

Work the first half of the stitch, but instead of completing the stitch, work the next half stitch and continue to the end of the row. The cross is completed on the return journey.

PRACTICE PIECE

Using a small piece of fabric, work the little test design shown in Fig 8. Depending on your fabric, experiment with the number of strands on your needle, so that the fabric is covered, but remember that some holes will be occupied by part of four cross stitches and you do not want to distort the fabric.

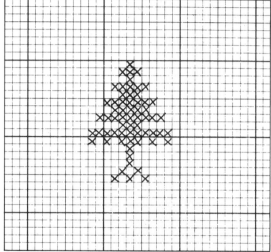

Fig 8 Practice piece of cross stitch

WHERE TO START

At last you are ready to start and you are faced with a plain piece of fabric and a chart with a design on it.

Don't panic; follow these instructions and you will see just how simple it is:

1 Lightly press your fabric and fold into four.
2 Open out and stitch a line of tacking stitches along the creases following the threads (see Fig 9).
3 Check that you have all the colours you need (for organiser see Fig 3).
4 Mount all the colours on the card with their shade numbers marked.
5 Sew a narrow hem or oversew to prevent fraying. This can be removed on completion.

BEGINNING

You will generally begin in the middle of the fabric and proceed outwards to-

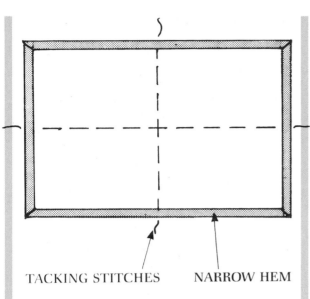

TACKING STITCHES   NARROW HEM

Fig 9 Hemmed fabric with the centre marked by lines of tacking stitches

wards the border. Look at your chart, find the middle and check which colour is used. Thread your needle and place the first cross stitch on the fabric where the lines of tacking threads cross. At this point you have to decide in which direction to work. It is probably the best policy to work towards smallish gaps, as counting over large areas of blank fabric can be nerve racking.

You will no doubt develop techniques of your own whilst sewing, but here are some tried and tested hints.

THE GOLDEN RULES

1 Always work with clean hands
2 Never work while wearing fluffy woollen jumpers
3 Keep the work wrapped when not in use. (Pillow cases take an average size frame easily.)
4 Mount colours on an organiser and identify the make and shade number
5 Check that you have enough thread to finish the project as dye lots vary
6 Sew a hem around the fabric to prevent fraying
7 Do not use knots to anchor the stitches
8 Work from the centre to ensure an adequate border for stretching and framing
9 Do not travel between areas of colour unless the thread can be hidden behind existing stitches
10 Never have coffee or other drinks near your work
11 Finish off the ends as you go. Do not leave them all to the end.
12 The cross stitches should all be worked in the same direction with the top stitch facing the same direction.

CHAPTER 3
FIRST PROJECTS

These early projects are designed to demonstrate the basic skills required and for you to have some finished work to inspire you.

Bookmarks are always lovely presents for any age group and when worked by hand are particularly precious. One of the designs has been adapted to fit a simple greetings card to show how easy it is to alter simple motifs to suit your requirements.

Cottage Bookmark

This simple cottage is stitched on a coarse linen with a slight oatmeal texture. The design is worked in autumn shades to complement the colours in the fabric.

Stitch Size: 48×14
Design size: 7×2in (175×5cm) (size of bookmark)

MATERIALS

linen in natural shade: 18 threads to the inch
narrow brown ribbon: 6 – 8in (15–20cm) approx
stranded cottons: use two strands for the cross stitch
    0263 – dark green
    0375 – dark honey
    0337 – peach
    0372 – honey
    0341 – rust
    0355 – rich brown

INSTRUCTIONS

If about to panic here, refer to the golden rules on p15.

Lightly press the fabric, fold in four, and stitch the tacking lines as described on p14. Look at the chart and find the centre stitch, which in this case is worked in 0337 – peach. Thread your needle with the right colour and place your first stitch where your tacking threads cross. Work the six cross stitches that make up the front door, finish off the ends (see Fig 10) and snip off the threads as close to the fabric as possible. Following the colour chart, work the walls of the cottage and finish off as before. Now you can decide in which direction you wish to proceed. Either work the roof and chimneys or work the fence either side of the cottage.

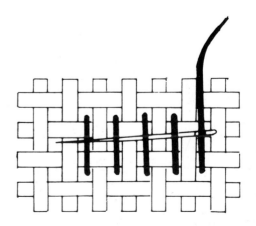

Fig 10 Finishing off the ends at the back

Bookmarks and Greetings Card

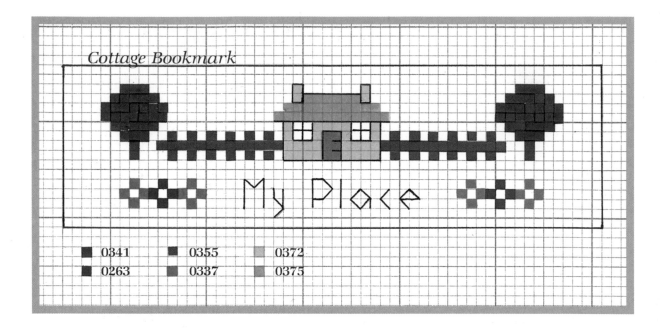

Cottage Bookmark

■ 0341   ■ 0355   ▨ 0372
■ 0263   ■ 0337   ▨ 0375

When the cross stitch is complete you can start to add the outline. Always add the outline after the cross stitch to keep the lines crisp and even.

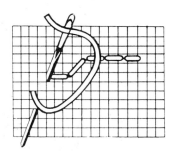

Fig 11 Back stitch on linen

The outline is worked in one strand of 0357, and in back stitch (see Fig 11). The back stitch is worked over two threads of linen, thus sharing holes with the cross stitch.

To work 'My Place' in back stitch, start with the top of the letter 'P' and work in each direction until the writing is complete. The threads can be carried across the back of the work, and finished off when the writing is finished.

Continue with the cross stitch until the design is complete and then lightly press on the wrong side.

MAKING UP

As illustrated in the colour photograph this bookmark has a frayed edge which is very simple to do. Decide how much border you need. Using a toning thread, work a line of back stitch around the design (see Fig 11), fray the edge to back stitch, and trim to neaten the edge.

If you wish to add the ribbon, as in the worked model, tack in place and the back stitch will anchor it in place.

Greetings Card Version

Cards especially designed for craft work are available from most good needle-work shops and make lovely gifts. The cards are usually three-fold cards (see Fig 12) and a rubber based adhesive can be used to fix the needlework in place.

Tower Block Bookmark

This is just a modern version of a traditional idea and great fun. This design would make a lovely spectacles case – especially for a confirmed city dweller.

Stitch count: 82×26
Design size: 6×2in (15×5cm) (bookmark, not including the lace)

MATERIALS

aida cloth in white: 18 blocks to the inch
blue ribbon: 4in (10cm) approx
narrow white lace: 24in (61cm)
cotton lace motif × 1
stranded cottons: use one strand for the cross stitch

INSTRUCTIONS

Select a piece of aida fabric and oversew the edge to prevent fraying. Work the design as previously explained, using just one strand of cotton for both cross stitches and the outline. With this design, it is probably easier to follow the chart if the cross stitch on each building is completed before moving on.

When the design is finished, press lightly on the wrong side and pin the lace around the edge of the fabric, starting at the centre of a short side. Pin the ribbon and the motif over the join and tack in position. Using matching white thread and using back stitch, sew through all the layers. This could be done on a sewing machine if so wished.

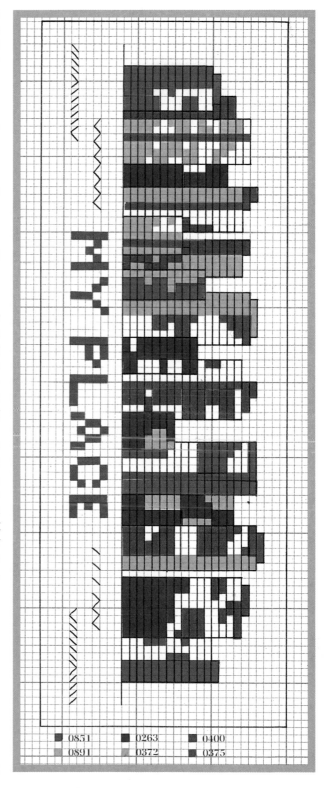

■ 0851	■ 0263	■ 0400
0891	0372	■ 0375

Tower Block Bookmark

New Home Card

What a lovely surprise this little card would be on that most exhausting of days!

Stitch count: 32×28
Design size: 2½×2in (6.25×5cm)

MATERIALS

linen in ivory shade: 26 threads to the
　inch
stranded cotton: use two strands for the
　cross stitch
　0263 – dark green
　0372 – honey
　0355 – rich brown
　0378 – dark stone

INSTRUCTIONS

Using the chart (Fig 13), adapted from the bookmark, work as before.

Lightly press the picture on the wrong side. Unfold the card and carefully position the opening over the needlework. Trim away any excess fabric making sure you leave enough to stick to the card.

Open out the card and cover the back face of the opening with a thin coat of adhesive. Stick down the fabric and the third fold of the card. Ensuring that no adhesive oozes out, place the completed card face down on a clean surface and cover with a book or a similar object until dry.

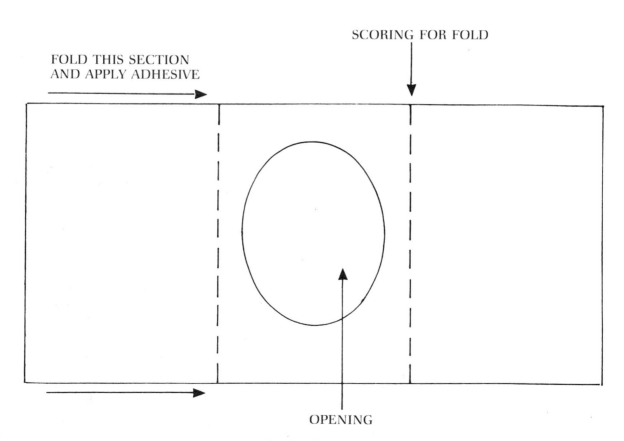

FOLD THIS SECTION
AND APPLY ADHESIVE

SCORING FOR FOLD

OPENING

Fig 12 A three-fold greetings card

for the house with the photograph and the fabric at hand, remembering that variety of colour can be achieved by mixing the shades on the needle (ie one strand of each of two different shades on one needle). Mixing the colours can be very effective for brick walls and plain roofs instead of large expanses of the same shade.

Any house can be translated to a cross stitch picture, although not all property can be described as picturesque. A little artistic licence can be used with strategically placed greenery and invisible down pipes.

Fig 14 Measuring the dimensions of the pincushion pad

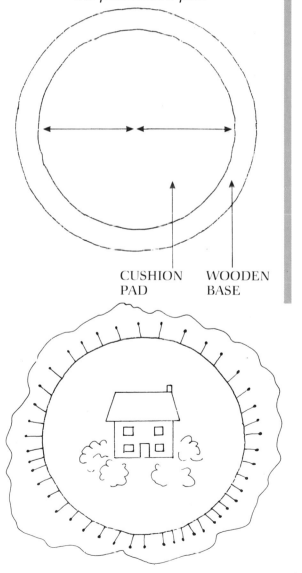

CUSHION   WOODEN
PAD   BASE

Inglestone Pincushion

Stitch count: 34×40 (including back stitch writing)
Design size: 2¾×3in (7×8cm)

MATERIALS

linen in sepia: 25 threads to the inch
pad and wooden base
assorted flower threads (chosen for this cottage for the matt texture).

INSTRUCTIONS

Work the cross stitch design as previously described, using one strand of flower thread or two strands of stranded cotton if you prefer. When complete lightly press on the wrong size.

MAKING UP

Gently press a pin through the middle of your design and then through the middle of the cushion pad, thus centring the picture. Using glass headed pins, secure the needlework along the base of the pad (see Fig 15) and, when you are satisfied with the shape and smoothness of the fabric, stitch invisibly through the needlework and the cushion pad. Remove all the pins and check for unnecessary folds and pleats. Only when you are completely satisfied, trim away any excess fabric leaving enough to tuck underneath. Add the base, tuck the fabric inside and tighten the screw provided.

Fig 15 Making up the pincushion

CHAPTER 4
PERFORATED PAPER DESIGNS

These novelties can be adapted for all sorts of purposes, as the perforated paper can be cut, folded, glued and stitched.

THE HISTORY OF PERFORATED PAPER

During the nineteenth century the art of perforated paper needlework was in its heyday. European ladies took classes in cutting and stitching techniques and extremely elaborate, often religious designs were produced.

In America the craft reached its zenith at the end of the nineteenth century with ladies' journals giving advice on the latest techniques.

The earlier perforated paper articles were often bookmarks with mottoes or verses of scripture embroidered in threads and beads. Later, visiting card cases, lampshades, comb cases as well as table mats and handkerchief boxes appeared.

Because the nature of the material used for these items was prone to damage over the years, antique examples are not easy to find. A perforated paper needlecase embroidered with roses and leaves recently fetched an amazing sum at auction.

HELPFUL HINTS

1 Although the paper is quite strong, do remember it needs to be handled with care.
2 There is a right and a wrong side to the paper, the smoother side being the right side.
3 Avoid folding the paper in any way. Find the centre with a ruler and mark with a pencil. Pencil lines can be removed with a soft rubber.

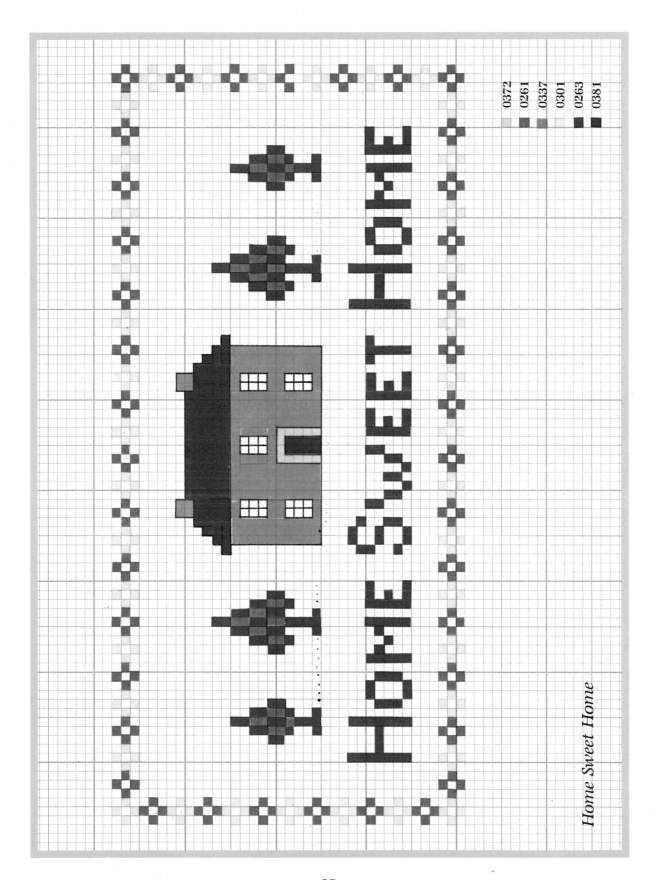

Home Sweet Home

Notebook Cover

This simple little design is very similar to the styles used during the Victorian era. It is made up as a notebook cover, but could easily be adapted to be used as a bookmark or wall hanging.

Stitch count: 84×39
Design size: 6×2¾in (15×7cm)

MATERIALS

perforated paper in sepia: 14 holes to the inch
stranded cottons as listed on the chart

INSTRUCTIONS

When using perforated paper, always give yourself a good margin of material as the paper is quite delicate and the perforations near the edge can tear when handled. It is easier to cut the paper as and when necessary. To find your starting position, count the holes and mark the centre by dropping a glass headed pin through to use as a pointer, or use a soft pencil. Using three strands of stranded cotton, work the design from the chart. Try not to bend the paper and always work with clean hands as the paper marks easily.

When the design is finished, trim away the excess fabric and cut a piece the same size.

To make the cord for the spine of the notebook cover, choose three coloured threads to tone with the design. In this case one strand of 0337, 0301 and 0261 were plaited together as evenly as possible and threaded through the spine of the booklet and two sheets of paper using a tapestry needle. Thus completed it was actually used as a visitors' book.

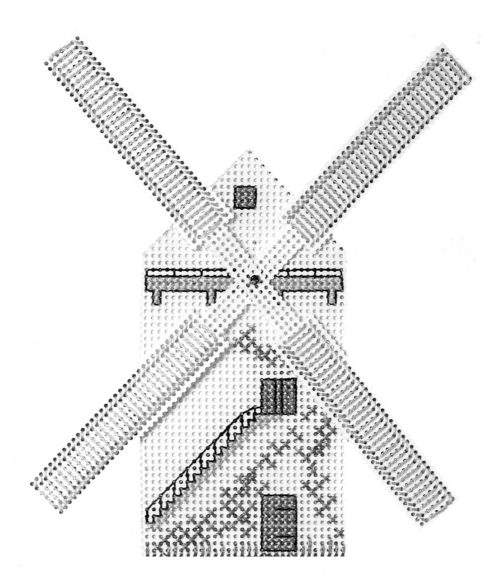

Windmill Card

This design was great fun. The sails of the windmill actually go round. A single sheet of perforated paper was used with a lining of fine card cut to fit and providing the second fold of the card. You may find when using this paper that as you cut you become even more inspired.

MATERIALS
perforated paper in ivory: 14 holes to the inch
assorted stranded cottons
one glass bead

INSTRUCTIONS
The windmill shape can be seen on the chart, with the stairs, the door and the balcony, but all the flowers were added free hand and at random although the colours are suggested. The grass at the bottom of the design has been worked in two strands of dark green thread in back stitch and the outline is stitched in one strand of black.

The sails are worked in half cross stitch and a few long stitches as in the diagram.

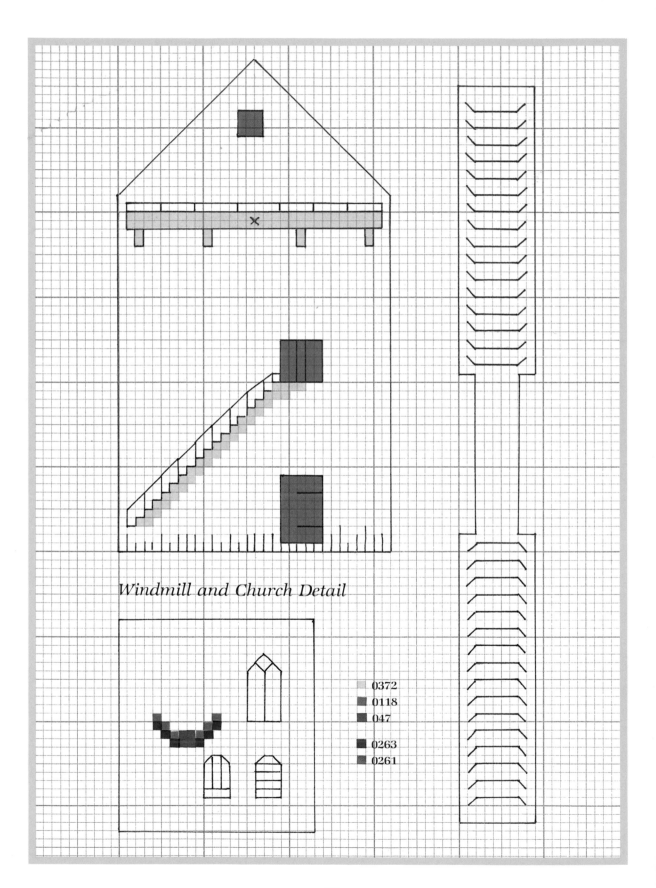

Windmill and Church Detail

0372
0118
047
0263
0261

When completed, place the mill flat on a clean surface and centre the sails, passing a glass headed pin through all the layers. Arrange the sails to your liking and stitch through all the sheets, removing the pin and adding one glass bead to the right side to prevent the paper tearing and to cover the stitches. To enable the mill to be used as a card you will need to make the backing card. Fold a piece of card in two and press down the fold firmly. Cut a mill shape on the fold and, using a rubber-based adhesive, fix this to the back of your sewing and allow to dry.

Christmas Tree Decoration

Perforated paper really lends itself to tree ornaments, the one illustrated being a very simple example. Many examples of Christmas novelties are charted and are available in good needlework shops as is the paper, in a variety of colours. Houses, fir trees, sleighs, presents and even holly leaves can be worked as table settings, tree ornaments or gift tags.

Stitch count: not applicable
Design size: as large or small as you like

MATERIALS

perforated paper in ivory: 14 holes to the inch
stranded cottons as listed on the chart (opposite)
a few glass beads in red and green

INSTRUCTIONS

Cut out the sort of shape you would like, leaving a margin as described before. As you will see from the picture, the roof of the church is worked in two shades of grey. To achieve this effect mix the strands on your needle to the shade you require. The snowy areas are worked in white and the leaves in dark green. To add a little sparkle, try mixing silver thread or white blending filament to the white cotton as you sew. All the outline (the window) is stitched in one strand of dark grey. The berries are simply red and green beads stitched in place using a half cross stitch.

When the design is complete add the hanging thread in silver or gold, covering the join with the addition of a few glass beads. If you wish to back the design to cover any rear view, proceed as for the windmill.

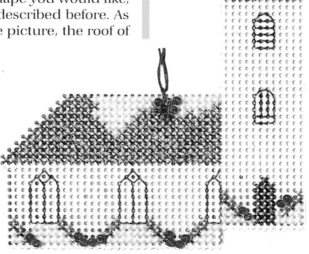

CHAPTER 5
FABRIC PAINTING AND CROSS STITCH

This chapter is for children of all ages. Playing with fabric paints and colour is a much underrated pastime!

As long as you are prepared to adapt your ideas to suit any unusual printing, stencilling or flecking results you obtain, you may be pleasantly surprised by your own efforts.

The rules are easy to remember:
1 Do not do this in a hurry
2 Cover all surfaces, particularly yourself, because the paint goes everywhere
3 Use proprietary brands of fabric paint and then follow the instructions on the pot
4 If it says 'wait until completely dry' do as you are told!

30

Sandcastle Fort

This little piece of nonsense is a cross between a sandcastle and a fort and could be adapted for T-shirts, shoe bags or kept just as a picture. The sample in the photograph is waiting for a little hand print and an initial from its owner.

Design size: 9×7in (23×18cm) (from the extremes of the design only)

MATERIALS

aida in cream: 14 blocks to the inch
fabric paints: 'Setacolour' (made by Pebeo in France) paints were used for all the designs in this chapter, except the lighthouse, which was worked in silk fabric
stencil brush
graph paper
stranded cottons as listed on the chart
masking tape
craft knife

INSTRUCTIONS

Draw a simple castle shape on a piece of graph paper (actual size) which will then be used as a stencil for the paint. Using a craft knife, carefully cut out the shape, remembering that it is the hole you are going to use *not* the cut out.

Lay the stencil over the aida fabric exactly where you are going to paint, and fasten with masking tape.

Now you are ready to mix the paints. Until you have some idea of the shades you want to achieve, try mixing colours in an old ice cube tray and then use it as a palette.

This particular brand of fabric paint (Setacolour) is colour-fast, but only if it has been fixed by a hot iron after it has been allowed to dry naturally. To stencil the design, just remember not to have too much paint on the brush at any time and work from the edges in towards the middle. Now you are on your own!

ADDING THE DETAIL

On the example in the picture, the castle was outlined in two strands of 0375, as was the flag pole. The portcullis and the outline of the soldiers were stitched in one strand of black in back stitch. The soldiers' buckles may be worked in yellow or in a gold metallic thread (see the chart).

Pier Scene

This novel design is worked on a 14-count aida which has been speckled in sand yellow and seaside blue all done with fabric paint and a toothbrush. Be warned; before attempting this, cover yourself and your surroundings with newspaper!

Mix the fabric paint as described above until you have the right shades of blue and yellow for the sea and sand effect.

Lay the aida fabric (14 blocks) on the covered surface and cover one half with a sheet of paper. Dip the brush in one of the colours and, using your fingers, flick the bristles so that the paint speckles the fabric. Remove the paper and cover the painted side and repeat the procedure with the other colour. When you are satisfied with the colour, leave the fabric to dry naturally and then fix with a hot iron.

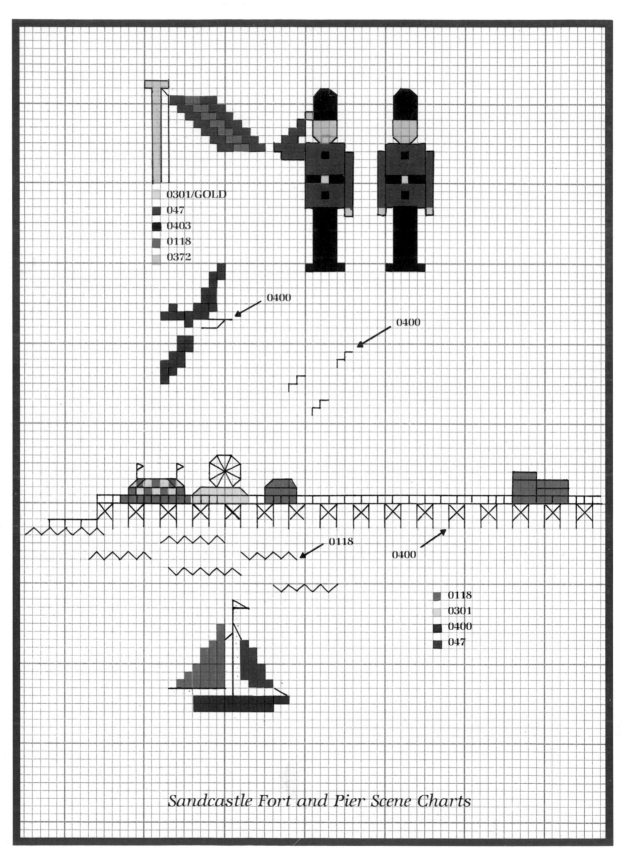

0301/GOLD
047
0403
0118
0372

0400

0400

0118

0400

0118
0301
0400
047

Sandcastle Fort and Pier Scene Charts

To complete the project, work the design in cross stitch (using two strands of cotton) from the chart opposite, adding the superstructure of the pier in back stitch using a single strand of black stranded cotton. The big wheel on the pier, the sea gull, the birds and the rigging on the boat are all stitched in one strand of dark grey. The waves in the foreground are stitched in one strand of the rich blue.

Potato Print

The little cottage photographed in the embroidery hoop was printed using potato shapes and the cross stitch added freehand afterwards. Children could have great fun with this sort of project because all the detail can be added afterwards with cross stitch. A lovely idea at Christmas is to print simple tree shapes and then add the decorations in cross stitch.

To make the printing blocks, wash, peel and cut the potatoes in half with a sharp knife, carefully drying the cut edges with kitchen paper. To print the designs, mix the paints as described in the previous project and experiment with some of the potato shapes to see what effects you can achieve. When you have finished printing the design on the linen (26 thread), leave it to dry before ironing with a hot iron to fix the colour. Using stranded cottons, add the details in cross stitch, french knots and back stitch.

Lighthouse on Silk

This picture has been included in this chapter because it involves fabric painting, although by an entirely different method to the earlier projects. The cross stitch is worked by using the waste canvas method (which will be explained in detail below) and is stitched on hand-painted silk fabric. Quite a few new techniques are included in this project and you may feel you need to have more experience before attempting them. Both silk painting and using the waste canvas method of counting cross stitch can add a new dimension to your work and can easily be incorporated into other projects in this and other books.

PAINTING SILK

Because of the very nature of silk, special paint and techniques have to be employed to ensure perfect results. If you intend to paint silk, always buy the correct paints, which are now readily available from needlework and craft shops.

MATERIALS

silk paints
gutta
fixative
needlework hoop
fine paintbrushes
stranded cottons as listed on the chart

INSTRUCTIONS

Gently iron the silk fabric with a warm iron and place in the needlework hoop, keeping the fabric as taut and as smooth as possible. The next step is to use gutta, which is a resinous liquid that forms a barrier to the paint when it is applied. Without the application of some sort of restraint the paint will run all over the fabric completely out of control. (The gutta will be washed out when the design is completely dry.)

To obtain the sea-like effect as seen in the picture, paint the gutta in wavy lines on the fabric and then paint the pastel shades of blues, greens and yellows.

When you are happy with the colour, leave the fabric to dry on a flat surface to prevent any of the paint running. When the fabric is dry paint over all the design with the fixative. (Follow the instructions on the bottle.) As soon as the fixative and paint are dry, the whole piece of silk should be washed thoroughly in warm soapy water to remove all traces of gutta and then left to dry naturally.

THE WASTE CANVAS METHOD

To enable the stitcher to work counted cross stitch on a fine fabric like silk, a piece of evenweave canvas or linen fabric is tacked on top of the silk and the stitches are worked through both layers (see Fig 16). When the cross stitch is complete, the threads of the top or 'waste' fabric are removed one at a time leaving the cross stitch behind. Clever!

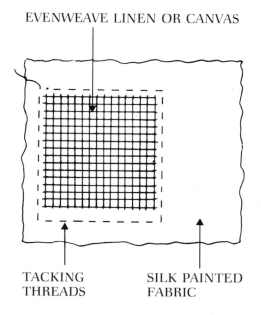

EVENWEAVE LINEN OR CANVAS

TACKING THREADS

SILK PAINTED FABRIC

Fig 16 The waste canvas method

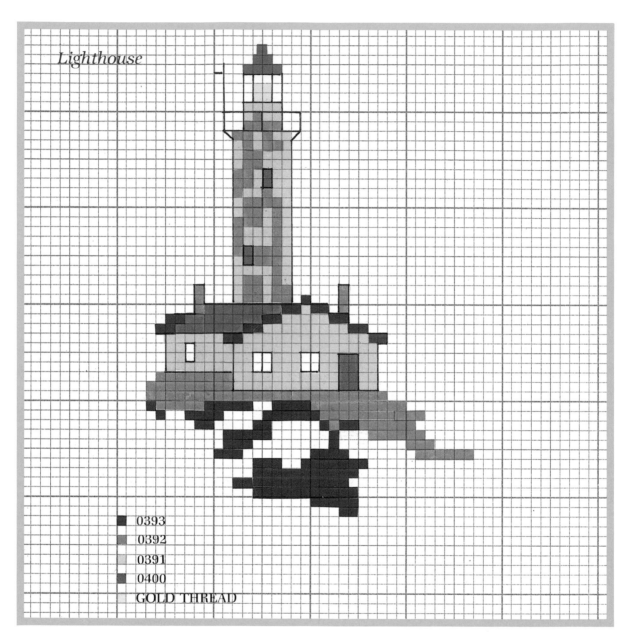

Lighthouse

0393
0392
0391
0400
GOLD THREAD

This basic technique can be used to embroider motifs on sweat shirts or baby linen or on almost anything.

ADDING THE DETAIL

To make the lighthouse in the picture, tack a piece of linen over one half of your newly painted silk fabric. Work the cross stitch by following the usual routine, using two strands of stranded cotton, but leave out the outline. Add the waves in cross stitch in colours to blend with your painted silk. The waves are stitched in free cross stitch around the base of the lighthouse.

Remove the threads of the linen carefully, one at a time until only the cross stitch remains, then add the outline in small back stitches in dark grey. Add a few random cross stitches amongst the painted waves and a single gold cross stitch for the light in the lantern.

When the design is complete, it may be stretched and mounted using a padded mount board and a traditional frame added.

Lighthouse on Silk

CHAPTER 6
DESIGN FOR YOURSELF

The two projects in this chapter are designed and charted to test your new-found designing and stitching skills As you will see, both charts are only included in part, with the layout and size of the projects left to you. The old brickwall writing case is an ideal project with which to start experimenting in the use of colour and shape as you need have little or no ability to draw or paint.

The wall was sewn on a pale mint green linen, lined in a matching polyester and cotton (bed linen) fabric with co-ordinating notelets and envelopes tucked into tailor-made pockets inside. There is even a tab to hold your pen in position.

The traditional sampler is based on a lovely village in the Cotswolds and is intended to inspire you to design and work a sampler showing one of your local features. A sampler does not have to feature a picturesque village scene – street maps, town centres, county maps, and even waterfronts have been included very successfully in contemporary samplers.

Writing Case

Writing Case

This design has been adapted to make a small writing case intended to hold little notelets and envelopes, but could easily be extended for use with any sort of writing materials. For this reason the design size for the model in the photograph is included, but the stitch count is not. When you plan your wall just make it wide enough and high enough to cover the front of your writing case.

Design size: 10¼×14in (26×35cm)

MATERIALS

linen in pale green: 26 threads to the inch
stranded cottons as listed on the chart
pelmet Vilene (a stiff, bonded interfacing material often used for tie backs, pelmets, lampshades etc; buckram, a woven interfacing could be used if you prefer)
dressmaking Vilene
polyester and cotton sheeting

INSTRUCTIONS

Once you have decided on the contents of your writing case you can calculate your fabric requirements. Choose the fabric most suitable for your design and cut the material to size. To do this, decide on the finished dimension of the front cover of the case, double this for the back cover and allow at least three inches all the way round for turnings. Work a narrow hem around the fabric to prevent fraying and then calculate the stitch count.

Lay the fabric face down on a clean flat surface, fold in half to form the writing case shape and tack along the fold. Using a ruler check the design size and the thread count and work out the stitch count:
ie design size × fabric count
  14in × 26 threads (13 stitches to the inch)
  14 × 13in = 182 stitches

Once you have the stitch count in both directions you can plan the design on a sheet of graph paper (use paper with ten little squares to one large one; it makes counting the stitches much easier). Draw a line around the required stitch count to act as a frame and away you go. As you can see from the chart, you can colour in the squares or use simple symbols to represent the stitches. Try drawing a simple wall shape to fill the width of the frame and add the little bits of detail, ie greenery, the stile, the letterbox and whatever else takes your fancy. The example in the photograph has a bit missing from the wall and a view through to some distant fields, complete with a few sheep. After adding the detail you can fill in the substance of the wall with one colour of crayon or a simple symbol even if you intend to jumble up the colours when you start to sew.

Before starting to stitch, go out and look at a few walls and you will see just how many shades of brown, grey, brick red and stone are in evidence. Then once you are sewing your imagination can run wild. When the cross stitch is complete, add any outline in a single strand of cotton in back stitch in a suitable colour, tie off any loose ends and lightly press on the wrong side.

MAKING UP

Although it is difficult to see from the photograph, the spine of the writing case is made by working five rows of four-sided stitch along the width of the fabric and then leaving this section unlined (see Fig 17). This soft spine allows for the thickness of the notelets and envelopes. In the example illustrated, all the four-sided stitch has been worked using threads pulled from the linen. This technique enables you to match the colour exactly and also provides you with a very strong yarn for the

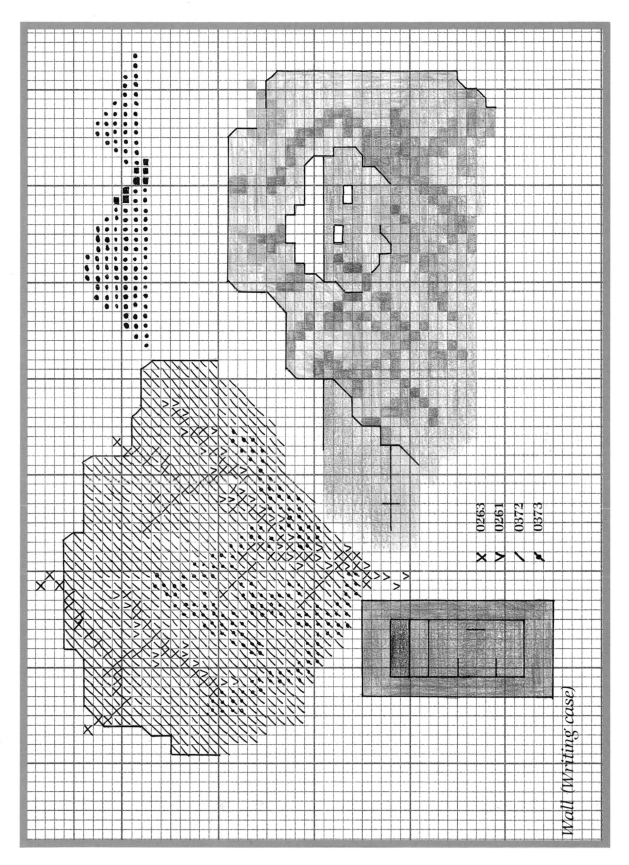

		0263
X		0261
V		0372
/		0373

Wall (Writing case)

finishing techniques. The threads should be pulled from each edge, one at a time, taking care to leave enough fabric for finishing. (You may take the threads from any spare pieces of fabric if you prefer.)

FOUR-SIDED STITCH

This stitch is usually worked from right to left and may be used for borders, filling and, as in this case, can make a very effective hem stitch. A four-sided stitch is actually three straight stitches to make three sides of a box with the adjacent stitch forming the fourth side (see Fig 18). The secret of success is to put the needle in at one corner and always come out at the opposite one pulling the thread tight, thus making a hole as you stitch. *No threads are actually removed for this stitch.*

Place the project, right side up, with the worked section towards you. Work the first row of four-sided stitches across your first line of tacking threads and then work a row each side until five lines of holes are complete.

Now work the hem, using the four-sided stitch as before, but working two rows. Work the first row of stitches exactly where the edge is to be formed, and then turn under the raw edges, making sure that the fold comes exactly along the line of squares formed by the stitches. Now work the second row through all the layers and through the same holes as the first line. When the edges are finished, carefully trim away all the excess fabric from the back and lightly press on the wrong side.

MAKING THE POCKETS

Lay the completed embroidery on a clean flat surface, right side down, with the worked section away from you. The worked section forms the lid of the writing case and will be dealt with in a different way to the base. Cut a piece of pelmet Vilene to fit the back section of the case and a piece of lining fabric the same size, but cut on the fold and allowing enough for turnings. Enclose the Vilene inside the lining and stitch invisibly with matching thread. Place in position in the writing case within the margins of the four-sided stitches and stitch in place. Follow the same procedure for the lid section, but use a firm dressmaking Vilene to give a softer, less rigid finish.

Cut pieces of pelmet Vilene to form the pocket shapes for the envelopes, the

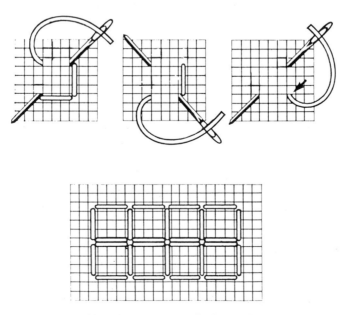

Fig 18 Four-sided stitch

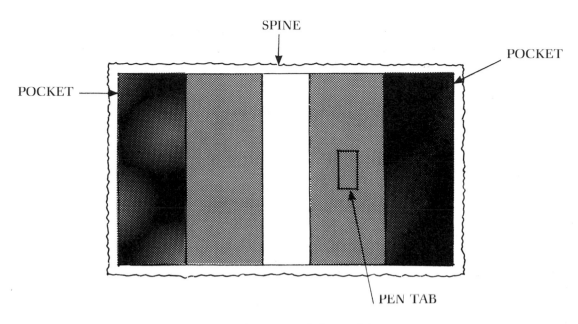

SPINE

POCKET

POCKET

PEN TAB

Fig 17 Inside view of the writing case

notelets, and a strip for the pen holder. Cover these in lining fabric as described above and position carefully inside the case (see Fig 17), and tack in place. When you are satisfied with the position of all the items, stitch in place using tiny hem stitches.

Now all that remains is to add the notelets, envelopes and a suitable pen and this lovely project is complete.

Village Sampler

The sampler illustrated in the picture is worked on an unbleached linen using stranded cottons and is based on a local village. As you will see the colour chart for this project is not complete so you will need to do some planning. A section of the border has been included showing how to turn a corner and, again, you will need to work out the rest for yourself (a pair of mirror tiles, hinged with clear adhesive tape, can be very useful here). The cottage, the shop and the post office are charted in colour and you could include buildings of local interest or even your own home (see p 22).

If you are going to plan your own design, use a good quality graph paper to plot the chart and remember that you may need to keep your chart for some time, so look after it!

Design size: 14×12in (35×30cm) (this dimension refers to the sampler in the photograph)

MATERIALS

linen in natural shade (unbleached)
stranded cottons as listed on the chart (model illustrated used two strands for the cross stitch)

ILLUSTRATIONS

Draw out the border of your choice making sure that the two ends meet. Using a soft pencil, draw in your centre lines and possibly the diagonals as well; these can be very helpful when placing buildings and when trying to end up with a balanced effect (see Fig 19). The tacking lines are also useful when checking the margins between the individual motifs and the stitched border. At this point it might be useful to refer to the sections on choice of fabric and threads and refresh your memory about where to start. As you stitch you may wish to change some of your plans, so keep an open mind and remember that the chart should be only a guide and can be changed and adapted to suit your taste.

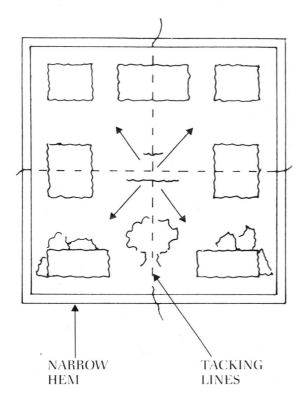

NARROW   TACKING
HEM   LINES

Fig 19 Planning chart for a sampler

Village Sampler

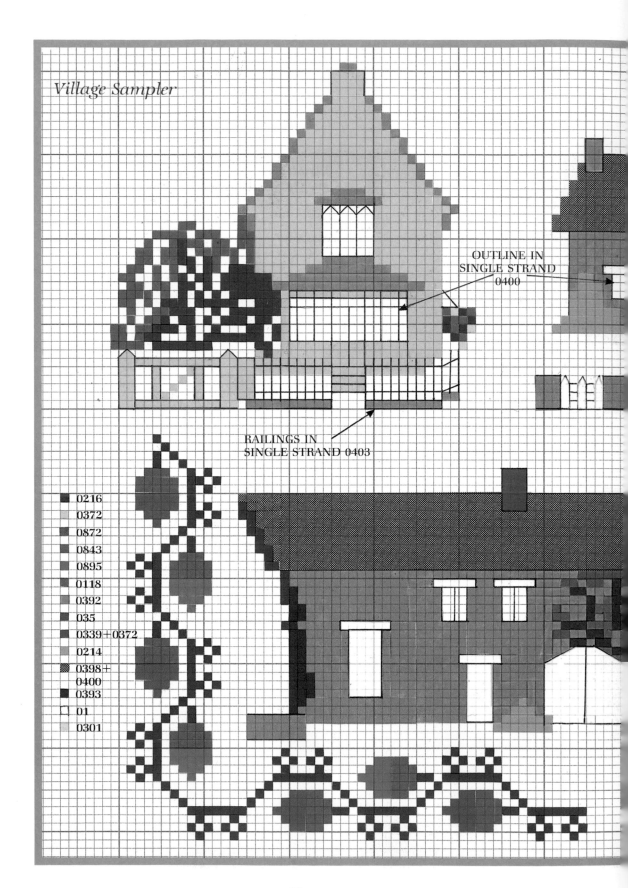

Village Sampler

OUTLINE IN
SINGLE STRAND
0400

RAILINGS IN
SINGLE STRAND 0403

0216
0372
0872
0843
0895
0118
0392
035
0339+0372
0214
0398+
0400
0393
01
0301

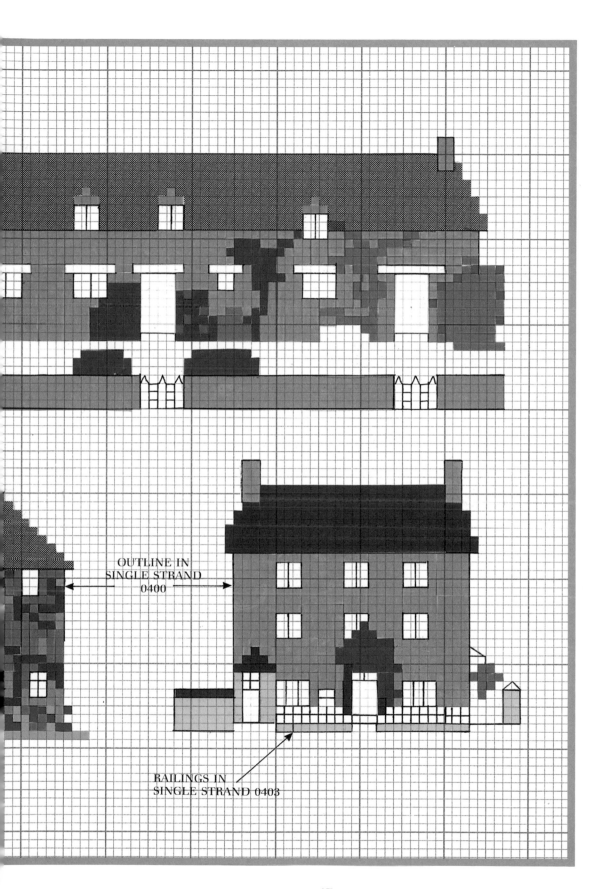

OUTLINE IN
SINGLE STRAND
0400

RAILINGS IN
SINGLE STRAND 0403

CHAPTER 7
VICTORIAN SCENES

These three Victorian scenes have created three completely different atmospheres, from the homely Victorian Terrace to the grand and gracious Victorian Conservatory. The Rose Bower shows how a very simple design executed in a few carefully chosen colours can be just as effective as a more elaborate piece.

Victorian Terrace

This charming idea is adapted to make a needlework purse and needle case, but could be used for a handkerchief case. Another way of using the design in the same format would be to adapt to a travel jewellery case.

The houses have been stitched in stranded cotton and silk thread on a plain single canvas. The beauty of this design on canvas is that the background is left unstitched which adds a pleasant effect. To add texture a few french knots have been included, and mixed threads have been used to enhance the larger plainer areas.

Needlework Purse
Stitch count: 90×55
Design size: 7¾×5in (19.5×12.5cm)

MATERIALS

single canvas in ecru: 14 stitches to the inch
stranded cottons as listed on the chart
Designer Silks
purple 7×1 skein
red 5×1 skein

INSTRUCTIONS

Before you start the actual stitching you need to mark out the canvas to make sure it will be possible to make it up as portrayed in the colour photograph. It is worth spending time at this stage to ensure that you work the design in the right place.

Fold the canvas into three equal sections and press lightly with a warm iron. Sew a line of tacking stitches along these folds (see Fig 20). The design is worked on the front of the folded envelope shape as shown in the diagram. Work a vertical and a horizontal line of tacking

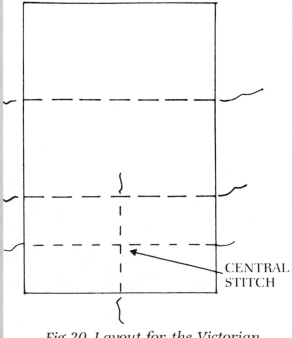

CENTRAL STITCH

Fig 20 Layout for the Victorian needlework purse

48

stitches across this front section to mark the position of the central stitch. The terrace is worked over one thread of canvas with three strands of stranded cotton or two strands of Designer Silks.

Each house is worked in a different colour in cross stitch with the roofs in mixed shades of grey. To obtain the shaded effects as seen in the photograph mix the threads in different combinations, ie two strands of dark grey and one of light grey or the reverse.

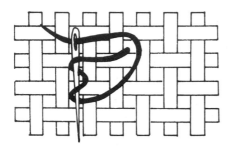

Fig 21 French knots

Add the french knots in three strands of Designer Silks, and the outline in two strands of dark grey stranded cotton after the neighbouring cross stitch has been worked. When the embroidery is complete, press lightly on the wrong side using a damp cloth. Using a blocking board, pull to shape, pin, and leave to dry.

MAKING UP INSTRUCTIONS

Before making up the design, cut a piece of interlining and carefully tack this to the wrong side of the worked piece, trimming the edges to match. The worked model in the picture is lined with the same canvas, but any lightweight fabric in a matching colour would be suitable. The whole piece is fully lined before the terrace is made up into the purse, so proceed as follows.

Fold the edges of the fabric inside, leaving one row of threads on either side of the design (see Fig 22) and place the lining fabric (raw edge turned in) wrong sides together, and pin in position. Carefully stitch the two pieces together,

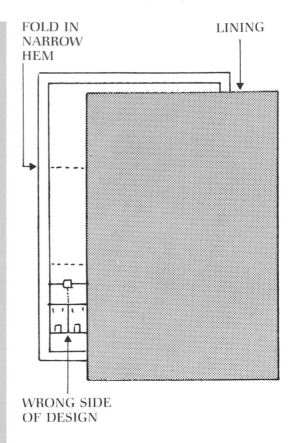

Fig 22 Lining the needlework purse

edge to edge, using a strong linen thread. Gently press the seams and fold up the bottom section to form the purse, pinning carefully. Stitch the side seams with linen thread, finishing the ends neatly.

Needlecase

This is a small version of the main design slightly adapted to fit the needlecase, using two of the cottages from the chart. When the cross stitch is complete, make up the cover of the needlecase as above. The pages for the needles were made out of a spare piece of natural linen cut with pinking shears, but a piece of flannel would be more traditional (if a little difficult to find). A plaited length of stranded cotton is used to stitch the two together and to form the bow on the outside.

can be borrowed and used for appliqué. Borders of assorted leaves can be transformed with the addition of fabric flowers or even beads.

MATERIALS

linen in ivory: 28 threads to the inch
stranded cottons in two shades of green and one of black
red ribbon roses (or ribbon to make them)

INSTRUCTIONS

Using the colour chart, work the cross stitch in two shades of green (using two strands of cotton). This is a good design to try using two needles threaded with different colours and thus save changing threads all the time (see Fig 23).

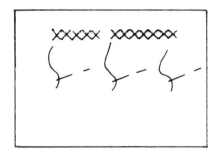

Fig 23 *Using more than one needle at a time*

The outline of the bower is stitched in back stitch in one strand of black cotton using the chart and the cross stitch as a guide. The detail on the wrought iron gate is also worked in back stitch. When the greenery is complete you can plan how many roses to make and where to put them.

Making Ribbon Roses

MATERIALS

narrow ribbon: ¼in (5mm) wide (the examples shown were made from Offray Ribbon)
matching threads
sharp needle

INSTRUCTIONS

To make a firm centre to the rose, roll one end of the ribbon making a tube shape and sew a few stitches through all the layers to secure it firmly. To form the petals, fold the ribbon downwards so that it is now parallel to the tube (see Fig 24) and, using the tube as a base, roll the tube across the fold loosely at the top and tightly at the bottom to form a cone shape. Sew a few tacking stitches at the base again and repeat the procedure until the rose is the shape you require, ie continue to fold, roll and tack, shaping as you go. To finish the rose, tuck the raw edge underneath and stitch into place.

When you have made enough flowers, experiment with various positions and, when you are satisfied, stitch the blooms invisibly amongst the greenery.

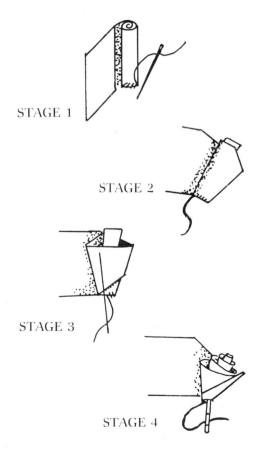

STAGE 1

STAGE 2

STAGE 3

STAGE 4

Fig 24 *Folding and stitching ribbon roses*

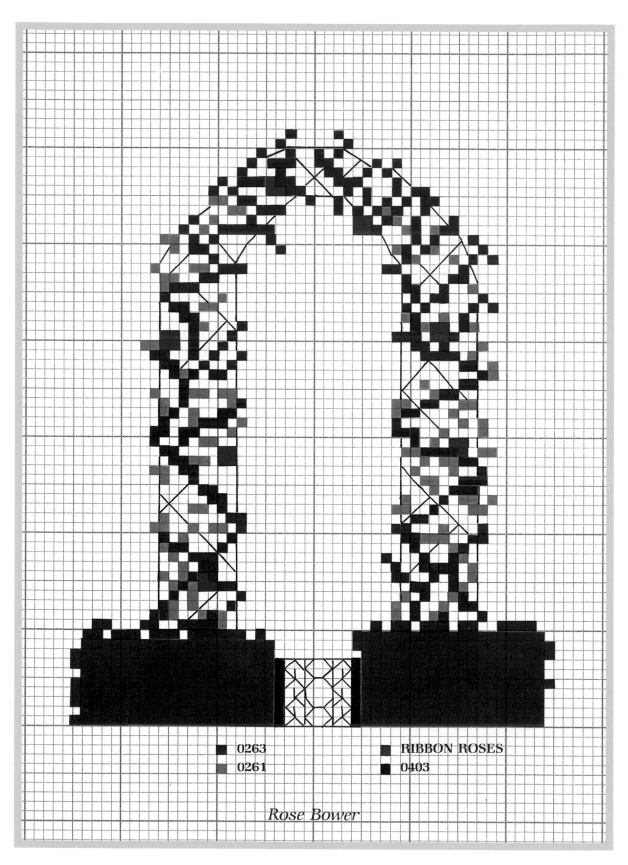

0263
0261
RIBBON ROSES
0403

Rose Bower

Victorian Conservatory

This lovely design is a mixture of counted cross stitch and free embroidery, linked together by the backdrop of arched windows. Apart from making a framed picture, the design could be adapted to make a lovely present for a keen gardener, perhaps as a diary or notebook cover. The picture can be adapted to make a larger design by repeating the arched windows from the diagram provided.

The idea of adding a conservatory to a book on castles and cottages is really a bit of self indulgence on my part, as I felt these lines from (*Punch* 19 January, 1987) 'A Winter Garden' summed up the need to have greenery around us whether in a cottage or castle!

> Though frost the broad gravel path
> hardens,
> The glasses are beaded with dew,
> Though it's desolate out in the
> gardens,
> There's life in the greenhouse at Kew.

The charted illustration shows one arch completed and one with open doors in the centre to create an illusion of a distant view.

The design in the colour photograph is worked on linen with a colour wash in water-colour in soft greens and blues to give an illusion of distance.

All kinds of threads have been used (an excellent project to use up oddments) so feel free to improvise! Stranded cottons, knitting wools, fashion yarns, felt appliqué, beads and silk threads in assorted shades of green could all be included.

stitch count: 69×43 (of design illustrated)
Design size: 5½×3½in (14×9cm)

MATERIALS

linen: 25 threads to the inch
water-colour paints
stranded cottons in
   greens, 0261, 0263, 0218, 0843
   honeys 0372, 0373
   scarlet 039
perle cotton in assorted greens
silk thread in sky blue

INSTRUCTIONS

Before you start your design, decide how many arches you are going to stitch, so that you can calculate how much fabric will be needed (see p 11). This design is intended to stretch your imagination and colour sense, so only guidelines are given (based on the model worked for the photograph).

Cut the linen to the required size, hem the raw edges and wash the fabric in warm soapy water (see p 11). This is to ensure that all the dressing added during the manufacturing process is removed before painting. When dry, iron the linen to remove all the creases and tack the centre lines as usual. Stretch the fabric onto a circular frame large enough to accommodate all the design, and you are ready to add the colour wash.

Using water-colour paints, spotlessly clean brushes and a clean saucer or similar container, mix soft shades of blues and greens. It is always better to start with pale colours and add more paint when you see how the wash looks on the fabric as it may be difficult to remove afterwards. If you are not sure about the result allow the linen to dry and check the colours in daylight before proceeding.

Once you are ready to stitch refer to the chart (Fig 25) and consider where to

Victorian Conservatory

start. It may be easier to work part of an arch worked in a single strand of black stranded cotton and then add permanent features, eg sundial or fountain next, so that greenery can be added afterwards. Allow the picture to build up gradually adding different textures as you go. You may be surprised at how effective cross stitch, couching and french knots can look.

The chart includes some simple leaf shapes, which can be used for cross stitch or even as templates for appliqué. To cut the shapes out of felt or other suitable fabrics just trace the shapes and use them as a pattern.

To give the impression of distance and to add perspective to the view through the open doors the little wall and flowers have been worked over one strand of the linen with a single strand of cotton. To do this correctly you must complete each cross as you stitch, rather than in two journeys.

This is one of those projects that is difficult to know when to stop, and can get out of hand! When you are satisfied with the picture remove it from the frame and gently press on the wrong side, being very careful not to flatten all texture you have so carefully stitched. Once stretched and laced over card (see p 116), you can complete the item as you wish.

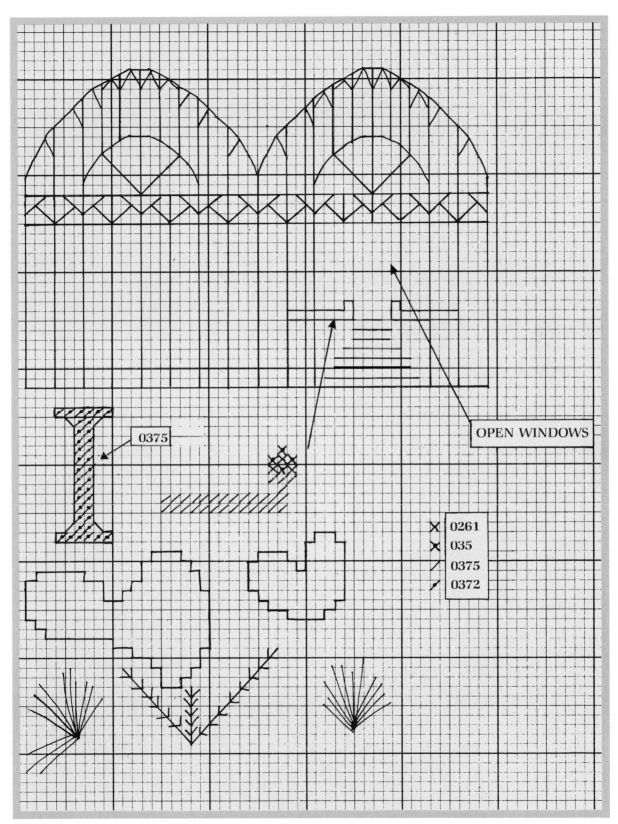

0375

OPEN WINDOWS

✗	0261
✗	035
╱	0375
✗	0372

Fig 25 Victorian conservatory

CHAPTER 8
CASTLES AND COTTAGES

Here are castles and cottages to suit every taste, plus a manor house, timber-framed black-and-white house, and even an oast house. The Windsor Castle project is shown in two versions to highlight the range of choices and effects available if you are prepared to be adventurous.

Mini Bell Pull

These four little designs are loosely based on some of the types of buildings you might see if you travelled east, west, north or south. An oast, a black-and-white house, a thatched cottage and a grey stone manor house are all worked in cross stitch in a vertical line to form the bell pull shape, which is finished with a small pair of brass ends.

The chart is designed with each building illustrated separately, and you could use them in any form. Each design could be used for pincushions, cards or even used to fill the lids of little trinket pots as seen on p 105.

To work them as a bell pull you will need to centre each design on your fabric as you stitch, so do ensure that you prepare the fabric before you start.

MATERIALS
aida in cream: 18 blocks to the inch
stranded cottons as listed on the chart
a pair of bell pull holders: 2½in (6.5cm)

INSTRUCTIONS
Follow the guidelines on p 11 to calculate your fabric requirements either by doubling this measurement to make the facing for the back, or by allowing two inches for turnings. Stitch a small hem to prevent fraying – this will be removed when the bell pull is made up. Fold the fabric into four, press lightly with a warm iron and carefully mark the centre folds with a line of tacking stitches.

In the photograph the thatched cottage is worked just above the centre line, so this is the example that will be described in detail. Before beginning to sew, examine the chart and count the coloured squares that make up the thatched cottage. Decide where the centre of the design is situated and place these stitches on the vertical centre lines just above the horizontal line of tacking threads. All the cross stitch on the worked model in the photograph was sewn using just one strand of stranded cotton with any detail added in one strand of a contrasting colour. If you decide to use a different type of material it may be necessary to increase this, so do experiment.

Continue to build up the design from the chart; centre each house as you work, leaving a margin of at least seven blocks of fabric between each one. When all the cross stitch is complete the phrase 'East, West, Home's Best' is optional – you may have ideas of your own here. The wording was stitched in

Clematis Cottage

This cross stitch picture is really just an extension of the bell pull projects, worked on a fine aida cloth using one strand of embroidery cotton. The model illustrated has been made up as a picture, but could be adapted to make a handkerchief case or even be set into a tea pot stand or tray. The beauty of working on a fine aida is that quite a lot of detail can be included because of the fineness of the fabric, and it may be easier on the eyes than a linen of the same stitch count.

MATERIALS

aida in cream: 18 blocks to the inch
stranded cottons as listed on the chart

INSTRUCTIONS

Stitch a narrow hem around the fabric and fold fabric into four. Press lightly; sew a line of tacking threads along the folds and place the centre stitch where the tacking lines cross.

Build up the design from the chart working out towards the edges. You may feel that you are ready to experiment and this is a good design to test your colour sense. Try turning this from 'Clematis' to 'Wisteria Cottage' by changing some of the colours on the house and in the garden and see how this affects the overall design. All the detail on this house is added in a single strand of dark grey after the cross stitch has been completed.

To prepare this picture for framing turn to 'Finishing Touches' p 116.

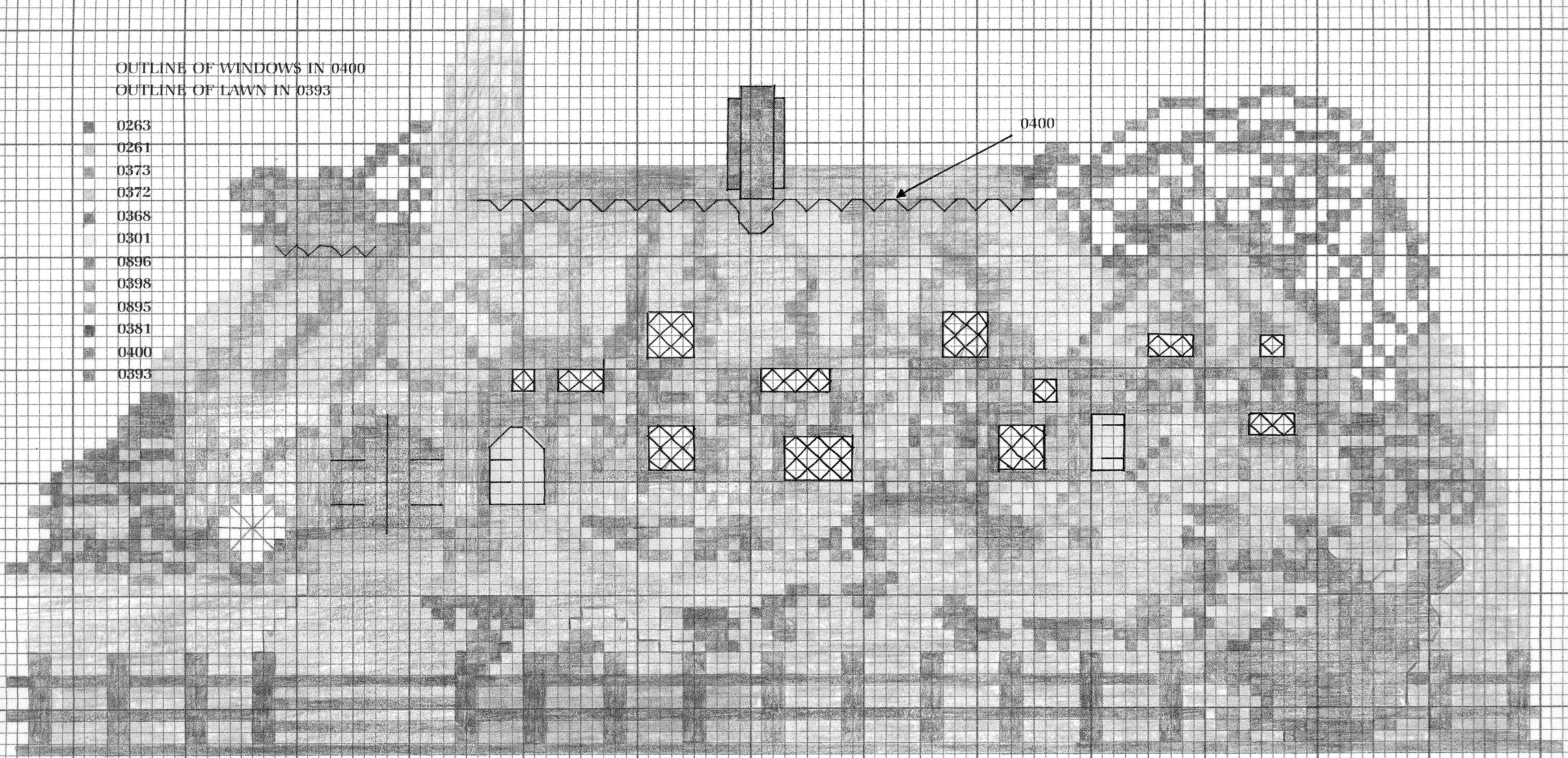

Clematis Cottage

ALL STITCHED IN SINGLE STRAND ONLY

OUTLINE OF WINDOWS IN 0400
OUTLINE OF LAWN IN 0393

0263	
0261	
0373	
0372	
0368	
0301	
0896	
0398	
0895	
0381	
0400	
0393	

0400

Windsor Castle

This famous castle is one of Queen Elizabeth's many beautiful homes in Great Britain and is often photographed from the view seen in the worked pictures illustrated here.

The design of the castle is worked in two different media to demonstrate how versatile counted needlework can be. One design is worked on aida with one strand of stranded cotton and the second version is stitched on canvas in fine Medicis wool using a half cross stitch only. The crewel wool is somewhat unusual as it has been over-dyed to give a shaded appearance without changing the yarn on the needle. This wool may not be easy to find, but instructions are given on how to obtain the same effect with other materials later in the chapter.

Cotton Aida Version

This example is a straightforward cross stitch picture, but it departs from tradition as the background is worked rather than left to show the fabric.

stitch count: 130×81
design size: 7¼×4½in (18×11cm)

MATERIALS

aida in ivory: 18 blocks to the inch
stranded cottons
0117 – pale blue
0892 – powder pink
0372 – honey
0399 – mid grey
0339 – rust
0262 – olive green
0373 – mid honey
0118 – mid blue
047 – red
0398 – pale grey
0400 – dark grey
0216 – sage green
0843 – lime green
0375 – dark honey

INSTRUCTIONS

This fine piece of work is stitched in just one strand of stranded cotton with the outline added in a single strand of dark grey.

Follow the chart, using the methods described in earlier chapters, but work the background sky in the palest blue. The river in the foreground is worked at random in assorted blues, greens and stone colours, although, to obtain the watery effect, you should work the stitches in broken rows as in the colour photograph. When the picture is complete, lightly press on the wrong side and stretch and mount as described later in 'Finishing Touches', p 116.

Wool on Canvas Version

This example is intended to give you some more ideas to develop your counted needlework skills. The same chart has been used for this very different effect using wool and canvas.

stitch count: as above
design size: 9×5½ (23×14.5cm)

MATERIALS

double canvas in sepia: 14 stitches to the inch
DMC Broder Medicis:
8208 – mid blue
8103 – pale peach
8400 – mid honey
8508 – pale grey
8103 – red
8419 – lime green
8301 – rust
8210 – pale blue
8322 – honey
8321 – dark honey
8507 – dark grey
8418 – sage green
8417 – olive green
dark brown stranded cotton for the back stitch outline

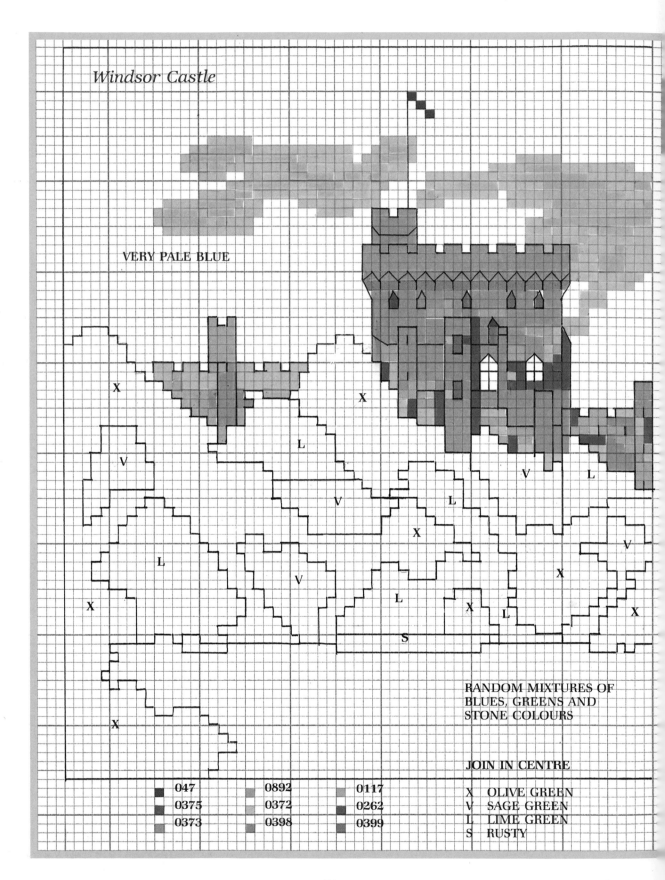

Windsor Castle

VERY PALE BLUE

X

X

V

L

X

V

V

X

L

V

X

L

L

V

X

X

V

L

X

X

S

X

X

RANDOM MIXTURES OF
BLUES, GREENS AND
STONE COLOURS

JOIN IN CENTRE

	047		0892		0117	X	OLIVE GREEN
	0375		0372		0262	V	SAGE GREEN
	0373		0398		0399	L	LIME GREEN
						S	RUSTY

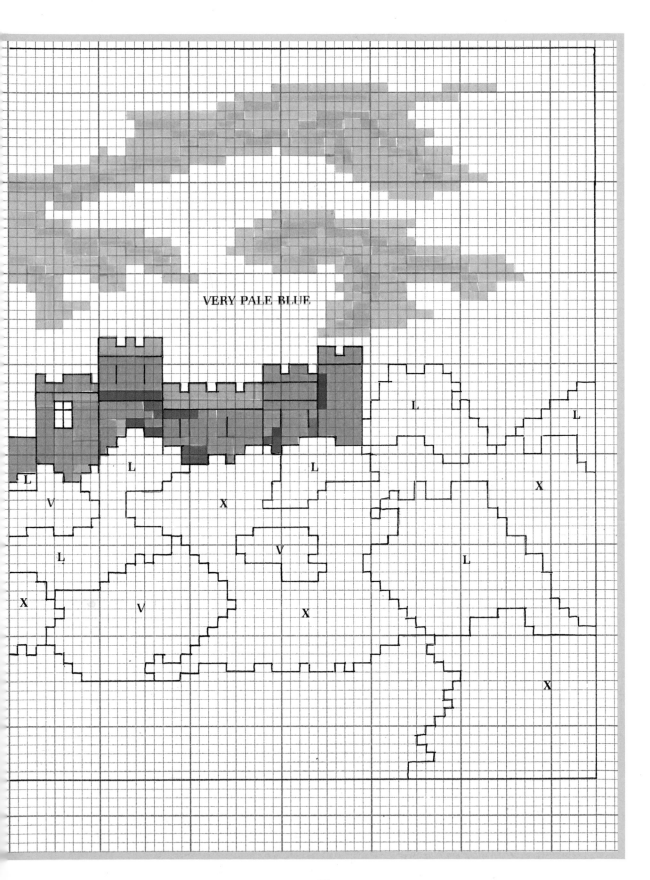

VERY PALE BLUE

INSTRUCTIONS

It is a good idea to work your canvas design on a rectangular frame, because all of the fabric is covered with half cross stitches which have a tendency to distort the material.

To prepare the canvas, check that the fabric has been cut along a line of threads. Follow the same guidelines as for linen (see p 11) to estimate the amount of fabric required and allow at least three inches all the way round. The edges of the canvas can be over-locked on a sewing machine to prevent fraying. A common practice seems to be to neaten the edges with masking tape, which is quick and easy, but can leave a sticky residue on the materials.

The half cross stitch (see Fig 27 and Fig 28) is worked in three strands of crewel wool and the outline is added in two strands of dark brown stranded cotton in back stitch when the castle is stitched.

To obtain the shaded look for the trees, try mixing some shades on the needle. Choose some more green yarns and sort them into the three groups as shown on the coloured chart, ie lime, olive and sage shades. When stitching the trees, experiment by adding a new shade to the needle, although keeping to three strands as before.

As with the fine version, work the water in the foreground with a selection of soft shades, working in broken lines to add dimension. When the canvas is finished, remove from the frame and carefully press on the wrong side, using a damp cloth. Stretching and mounting canvas is by a different method from that of linen and will be described in the relevant chapter later in the book (p117).

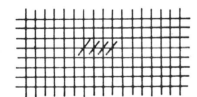

Fig 27 A half cross stitch on a single canvas

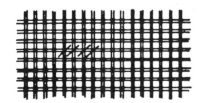

Fig 28 A half cross stitch on a double canvas

Windsor Castle

Fairytale Castle

This enchanting picture was inspired by an unforgettable visit to Disneyland, a trip planned for my children, but it would be difficult to know who enjoyed it more! Pure fantasy all day long.

The idea of using fairytales for cross stitch is one that can be extended further than just this castle. There are so many lovely characters that could be added to a fantasy series for some lucky youngster, using the same threads and textures.

The example in the photograph is particularly pretty as a sparkly thread was added to the stranded cotton to add that fairy touch. This unfortunately does not show too well in the picture, but is very effective in the original. As you will see from the photograph, the picture is in two parts, the design inside the mount and the clouds on the mount itself. This is quite simple to do and adds dimension and depth to the finished project.

It would be easy to adapt this pastel fairy castle to a grim giant's lair by changing the colours to muddy greys, blacks, and even reds to transform it completely. Try combining silver and gold matching embroidery threads instead of the blending filament.

stitch count: 127×80 (castle only)
design size: 11×9½in (28×24cm) (including mount embroidery)

MATERIALS

linen in dusty pink: 30 threads to the inch
stranded cottons as listed on the chart
silver machine embroidery thread
Balger Blending Filament (the magic ingredient)
shade 44 – turquoise/pink mix
shade 37 – pastel pink mix
shade 45 – lime-blue mix
a mount (mat board) with an oval opening measuring 9×6½in (22.5× 16.25cm)

INSTRUCTIONS

Before you start this project some decisions will have to be made regarding the end product. The most inexpensive way of buying oval mounts is to choose a ready-made size which can be bought over the counter. To have an oval cut especially for your finished piece will probably cost more than the materials for the needlework. Remember, the size of the mount quoted here was used for the design in the photograph, so you must check the thread count of your fabric to ensure that the design will fit.

All this may sound complicated, but it is not really. Refer back to 'How to calculate design size' on p 10 and the same rules apply. All you have to do is imagine that the purchased mount opening is the frame size and check that the design stitch count will fit inside it on your chosen fabric.

Once you are ready to start stitching, proceed as with any other cross stitch project, working from the middle and building up the design from the chart. The only difference is that all the cross stitches are worked in one strand of embroidery thread and one strand of blending filament. This special thread is a polyester-and-viscose mixture and feels almost weightless, thus not adding bulk to the stitch, but giving it a lustre that is most attractive. To obtain the colours as seen in the photograph, mix similar shades as you stitch, ie shade 37 with the pastel pink stranded cotton and so on. The effect is really pretty.

When the main design is finished, press on the wrong side with a warm iron and set aside whilst the mount is decorated. This is where you need to use your imagination.

Lay another piece of fabric out on a clean dry surface. It could be the same or a contrasting material so long as it is evenweave. Place the mount you intend to use face down on the fabric and lightly draw around the inside of the oval with tailor's chalk. Draw a line around the outside edge of the mount as well, then run a line of tacking stitches along the chalk marks, thus defining the area to be embroidered.

Using the chart as a guide only, try stitching the cloud shapes freehand, blending the colours as on the castle. As long as you stay within the defined areas, the design will fit on the mount.

There are two other projects later in the book which involve covering mounts, so the techniques needed to complete the castle are included there (see p 78).

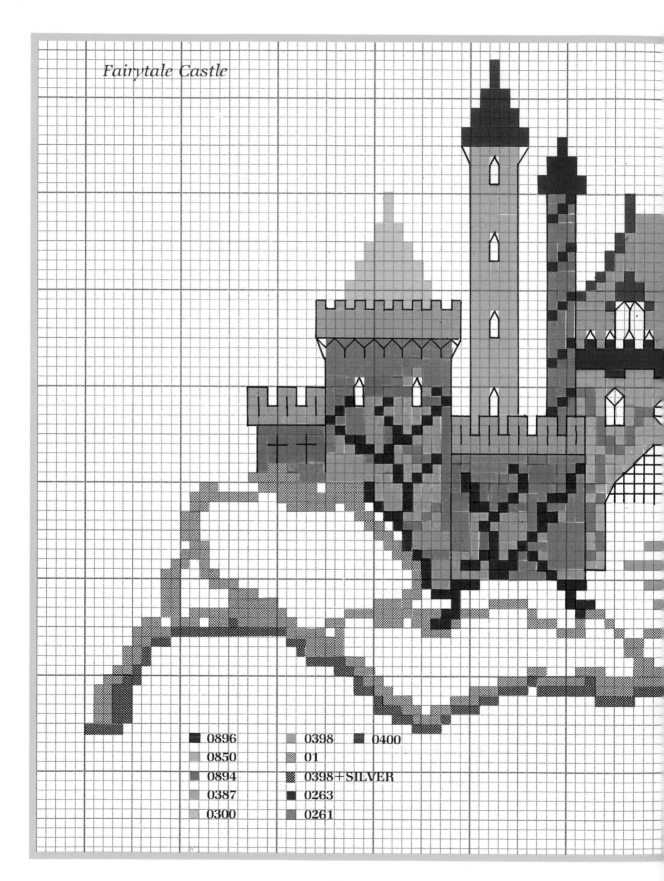

Fairytale Castle

■ 0896	▦ 0398	■ 0400
0850	▒ 01	
0894	▦ 0398+SILVER	
0387	■ 0263	
0300	0261	

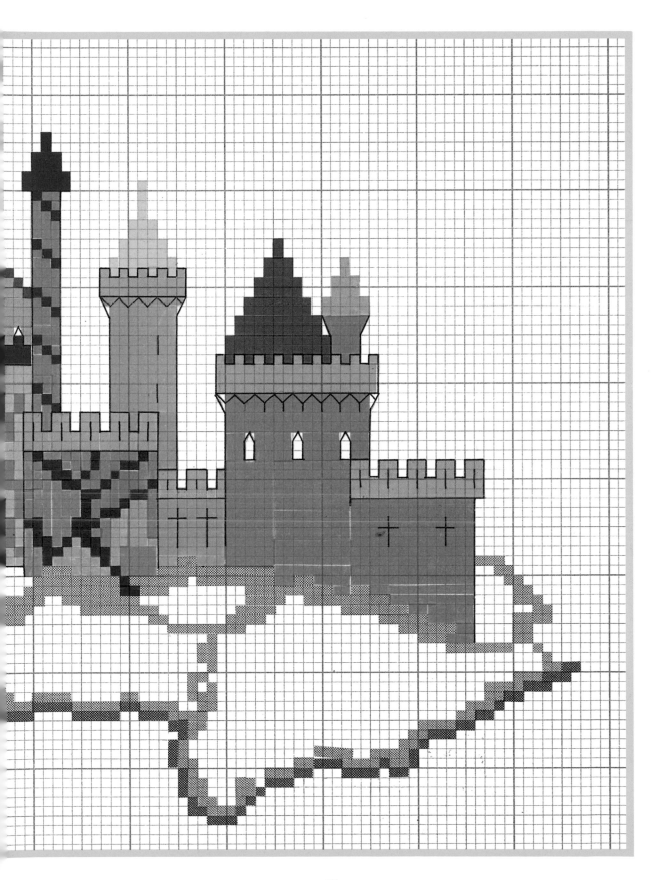

CHAPTER 9
WATER-COLOUR AND CROSS STITCH

Water-colour and cross stitch used together can produce the most rewarding results, as in these two charming scenes of a ruined castle and barn cottage. It is vital that the paint and stitching stages are kept separate, or paint will appear maddeningly in the wrong places. (See Chapters 5 and 10.)

Ruined Castle and Barn Cottage

These two pastel rural scenes were designed around a simple water-colour, adapting the cross stitch to suit the painting on the fabric. This can be best seen by examining the picture of the ruined castle. The fence to the right of the ruin has been stitched freehand to appear to enclose the hillock in the distance. This would be impossible to chart accurately because you may put your hillock somewhere else if you paint one at all. Therefore the charts for these two projects illustrate the buildings and immediate environs, but leave the position of the animals, greenery, vegetables and fences to you, the stitcher.

It would be perfectly possible therefore to leave out the painting altogether if you so wish and make up a design using any part of the chart and your own imagination.

stitch count: not relevant, as each feature will need to be counted to suit your painted linen
design size: 8×6in (20×15cm) (the design illustrated)

MATERIALS

(the same for both designs)
linen in ivory: 26 threads to the inch
water-colour paints
clean brushes
palette or similar receptacle
stranded cottons as listed on the chart (two strands of cotton used for cross stitch)

INSTRUCTIONS

Cut a piece of linen at least 8in (20cm) larger than your intended design size (ie 4in, or 10cm all the way round). Sew a narrow hem around the fabric because it may tend to fray as it will be handled more than usual. Before attempting to paint the fabric, wash it gently in warm soapy water to remove any dressing which may have been added during the manufacturing process. Allow the material to dry until you can iron out all the creases, and prepare to paint. At this stage it will help to use a hoop to keep the fabric taut whilst you add the colour.

Successful use of water-colour paints depends very largely on how little paint you use, ie the less you use, the more effective it can look. Mix up the colours

72

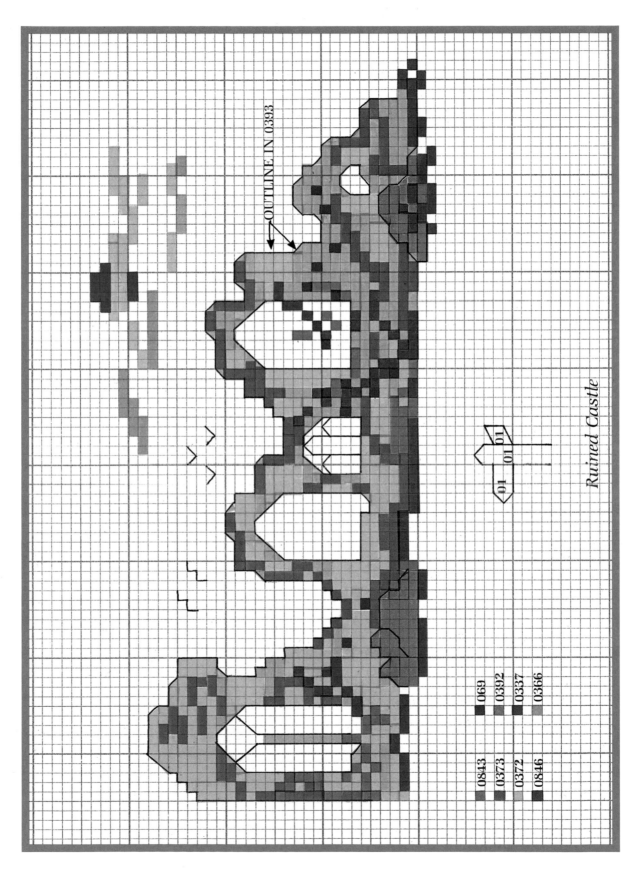

OUTLINE IN 0393

Ruined Castle

069
0392
0337
0366

0843
0373
0372
0846

01
01
01

Ruined Castle

Barn Cottage

74

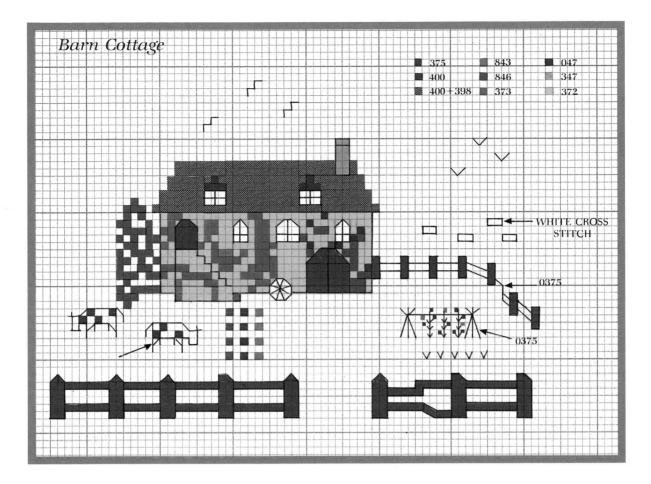

Barn Cottage

■ 375	▨ 843	■ 047		
■ 400	▨ 846	▨ 347		
▨ 400+398	■ 373	□ 372		

WHITE CROSS STITCH

0375

0375

you like and experiment on paper or scraps of spare fabric until you are satisfied with the result.

When the paint is quite dry, iron with a hot iron and sew the lines of tacking threads to mark the centre. You are now ready to start stitching. Before beginning a section of cross stitch, count that piece and check that it will fit where you want to put it. Greenery, animals and fencing can be added to suit the picture when you are ready, as can the birds and vegetable patch.

ADDING DETAIL

The outline on the ruined castle was added in one strand of 0393 as on the fence and the signpost.

The outline on the barn was stitched in one strand of dark grey as on the cows and the birds. The fence to the right of the house in the photograph was linked in back stitch in one strand of 0375 as were the bean poles in the garden. The little red flowers on the bean plants were worked in cross stitch but over just one strand of linen.

When the picture is finished to your satisfaction press lightly on the wrong side and mount ready to frame (see p 116).

CHAPTER 10
OVAL-MOUNTED PICTURES

These two quaint designs, Foxgloves and Rosewall, are rather like chocolate-box tops with traditional cottages, old English gardens and even water-colour in the background! The pictures in the photograph have been worked in two stages, the picture and the stitched mount, although you could work the whole design on one piece of linen or aida if you so wished.

Both designs are worked on the same principle, so these basic instructions are for both pictures and relate to the worked models in the photographs.

GENERAL INSTRUCTIONS

As discussed in the instructions for the 'Fairytale castle' the most practical way to attempt these projects is to purchase the mounts from art suppliers before you calculate your fabric requirements (see p 11).

For Foxgloves and Rosewall, two different linens were used to add contrast with a delicate pastel water-colour on the ivory fabric inside the oval.

CALCULATING FABRIC REQUIREMENTS

Once you have chosen the oval mount you intend to use you can calculate your fabric size. Measure the opening in the mount and then check the thread count on the material you intend to use for the main picture (see p 10 'How to calculate design size'). Once you are sure that the picture will fit within the opening, the material can be cut but make sure that it is at least 2½in (6.5cm) larger than the mount board. At this stage you can cut your fabric for the front of the mount and leave it aside for the present.

Before attempting to paint any linen fabric, wash it gently in warm soapy water to remove any of the dressing added during the manufacturing process. Allow the material to dry naturally, iron to remove all the creases and place in a suitable hoop keeping it as taut as possible.

FABRIC PAINTING

If you have no experience of using water-colour paints you may well surprise yourself. It is great fun and can be so effective. The secret is not to add too much paint at once and to take time to build up the picture.

Using spotlessly clean utensils and a clean work surface, mix pastel shades on a saucer and experiment on a piece of spare fabric or even a sheet of paper to see how the colours blend together.

Using soft greens and blues, paint the delicate tree and hill shapes on the fabric in the distance and the soft green in the foreground. Allow the paint to dry completely before removing from the hoop and ironing with a hot iron. At this stage decide which part of your painting you wish to use and which parts will be obscured by the embroidery.

Foxgloves

stitch count: 73×35 (within the oval)
design size: 9×7in (23×18cm) (including the mount)

MATERIALS

linen in ivory: 26 threads to the inch
linen in pale caramel: 26 threads to the inch
water-colour paints
oval mount with opening of 6×4in (15× 10cm)
stranded cottons as listed on the chart (two strands used for the cross stitch)

INSTRUCTIONS

You are now ready to begin stitching the main design, so proceed as with any other cross stitch picture – stitch a narrow hem to prevent fraying, tack the centre lines, identify the centre stitch and build up the design from the chart. When you have worked all the cross stitch, the outline of the house can be added in black, using a single strand only. The fence posts to the right of the house are worked in 0392 using two strands and the green plants in the foreground are worked in two strands of any dark green. The birds can be added anywhere above the house using one strand of black.

To decorate the mount proceed as follows: lay the second piece of fabric out on a clean surface and place the mount you intend to use face down on the top. Using tailor's chalk draw lightly around the inside of the opening and around the edge of the mount. Remove the mount and sew a line of tacking threads along the chalk marks, thus defining the area to be embroidered. Using the remainder of the design on the chart, work the foxglove and the small picket fence in cross stitch. The dark purple spots on the foxglove flowers are added in french knots (see Fig 21 p 50), after the cross stitch has been worked and the fence posts are linked in back stitch using two strands of 0392.

When both the house and garden are complete lightly press both pieces of work and set aside.

MAKING UP

You will need:
1 a pair of small sharp scissors
2 some double-sided sticky tape
3 a rubber-based adhesive like Copydex

METHOD

Place the mount face down on a clean work surface. Place a line of double-sided tape down the left hand side (this will be removed when the design is positioned). Cover the mount with the fabric, aligning the embroidery in the left hand corner and along the bottom. Using the sticky tape to prevent the design moving, turn the mount and the fabric over and place face down on the work surface. Check that you cannot see any of the stitches through the opening and adjust if necessary. Cut out the oval shape leaving sufficient for turning and sticking (see Fig 29). Clip inside the opening (see Fig 30).

Apply a thin coating of rubber-based adhesive to the curve of the oval and stick down the fabric (see Fig 31). Allow the glue to dry completely before removing the tape and stretching the outer edge of the fabric as described in the chapter 'Finishing Touches'. Before stretching and mounting the centre design to complete the project, lay the decorated oval you have just finished over the top of the cottage design to check its position and adjust this as necessary.

When both parts of the picture are mounted, a suitable frame can be purchased.

Fig 29 Cutting out the oval opening

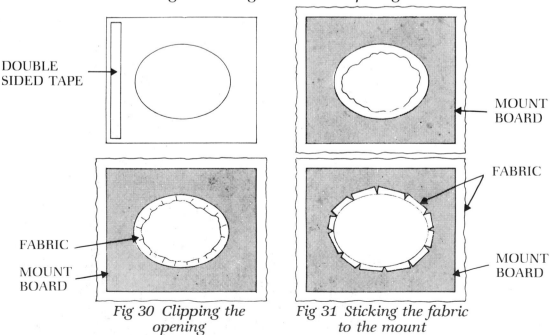

DOUBLE SIDED TAPE

MOUNT BOARD

FABRIC

FABRIC

MOUNT BOARD

MOUNT BOARD

Fig 30 Clipping the opening

Fig 31 Sticking the fabric to the mount

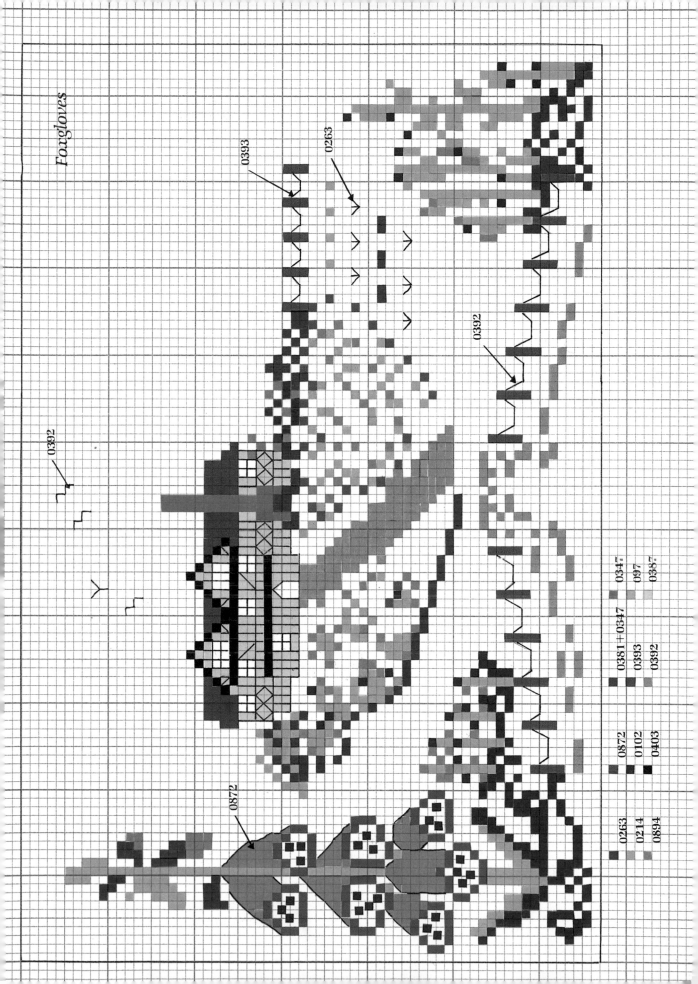

Foxgloves

0393

0263

0392

0392

0872

0263
0214
0894

0872
0102
0403

0381+0347
0393
0392

0347·
097
0387·

Rosewall

stitch count: 78×35 (within the oval)
design size: 9×7in (23×18cm) (including the mount)

MATERIALS

linen in ivory: 26 threads to the inch
linen in pale caramel: 26 threads to the inch
water-colour paints
oval mount with opening of 6×4in (15× 10cm)
stranded cottons as listed on the chart

INSTRUCTIONS

Work the cross stitch design from the chart after following the instructions given for 'Foxgloves'. When the cross stitch is complete, add the detail on the house with back stitch in the same colour as the front gate and the wall at the left of the cottage. The fence to the right of the house is added in one strand of brown and is intended to disappear under the mount when completed.

To stitch the embroidery on the mount, follow the instructions as for 'Foxgloves' and work from the chart.

You may notice that the worked design in the photograph is slightly different from the chart. On the chart, the wall to the right of the front gate is set back one stitch, but this was altered when the picture was stitched to improve the shape when the picture was framed, thus proving the adaptability of needlework charts.

When both parts of the design are finished, make up as for 'Foxgloves'.

Rosewall

0372	0895	0390	0104
0261	0896	0392	0301
0263	0375	0872	

CHAPTER 11
COLOURED FABRICS AND VIBRANT THREADS

The projects in this chapter are designed to illustrate the effect that can be achieved by using coloured fabrics and vibrant shades of rayon and silk, which add a rather Mediterranean flavour to the needlework.

The photograph album is a cross stitch design of a Greek fishing village, worked on dove grey linen and using brightly coloured silk and rayon yarns. The pages inside the book have been made from coloured art paper and a cord was made from matching stranded cottons. When the work is finished such a lovely album deserves first-rate holiday snaps.

The French house is worked on linen in a soft sepia colour, using stranded cotton – except for the flowers in the window boxes, which are worked in rayon threads to give colour and lustre and to act as a contrast to the dull, broken plaster of the house walls.

The Southern US house is worked on linen that has been soaked in tea, which gives the fabric a lovely musty colour. The design was stitched in three colours only, with added greenery for the trees. The project could be made up as a picture, a handkerchief box or a small jewellery case.

Greek Fishing Village
Photograph Album

Greek Fishing Village Photograph Album

As you will see this design is full of colour in the hope that it will remind you of hot sunshine and lazy days, when the winter weather closes in. It may look complicated but, like all cross stitch, if you work a section at a time, the picture will soon develop before your very eyes. There is no colour key for this project because it was stitched using oddments of silk, rayon and stranded cotton (an excellent design for using up bits and pieces). So long as all the threads are of similar thickness, the same effect can be achieved. The model in the picture is worked on a fine linen, but it would look just as effective stitched on a fine aida using single strands of stranded cotton.

stitch count: 133×88
design size: 12×9in (30×22cm)

MATERIALS

linen in dove grey: 30 threads to the inch (allow enough to cut a second piece for the back cover of the album)
assorted silk threads or stranded cottons for the buildings
white rayon thread
stranded cotton: 0393 for the outlines
acid-free card
matching lining fabric
coloured art paper for the pages
polyester wadding (for lightly padding the front cover)

INSTRUCTION

Cut a piece of linen at least six inches larger than needed for the design (to allow for turnings) and work a small hem to prevent fraying. Fold in four, press lightly and work the centre lines in tacking stitches.

Work the cross stitch from the chart, adding the back stitch outline after each section has been worked. This will help you to follow the chart more easily. When the picture has been completed, finish off any loose ends carefully and press lightly on the wrong side.

MAKING UP

Cut two pieces of acid-free card to the size of the finished album and two pieces slightly smaller for the lining. Also cut a strip for the spine of the book, the same depth as the album and about 1in (2.5cm) wide. The idea is to cover each piece individually using the embroidery and lining fabric, before assembling the album. To do this, cut out the lining fabric, using the two smaller card shapes as a pattern, and allow enough fabric for turnings. Using the strip of card as a pattern, either cut two pieces of lining or one piece of lining and one strip of the linen used for the embroidery. To cover the spine section, lay the card between the two pieces of fabric, turn in the raw edges and slip stitch around the long sides. Fold the ends to the inside and slip stitch carefully, making sure that the stitches do not show from the outside of the spine.

When mounting the embroidered front section of the album, a softer effect is achieved if the card is lightly padded, so, using the card as a pattern, cut a piece of polyester wadding slightly larger than the card and make up as follows.

Lay the card on a clean flat surface, place the wadding on top and lay the needlework on top of that. Check the position of the design and fold the excess fabric around the card, thus dragging the extra wadding over the edge to give a softer look. Lace the fabric over the card (see p 117) and check the position of the design as you proceed.

Cover the remaining pieces of card in

the same way and then the whole thing can be assembled quite simply. Lay the embroidered section and the back cover on a flat surface. Lay the lining covered sections on top, wrong sides together. Stitch invisibly around the edges, and make up as follows.

Line up the front, the spine and the back cover so that all the edges are level and stitch together using matching thread. A purchased cord could be used to hold the pages in place unless you wish to make a twisted cord from colours in the needlework.

MAKING A TWISTED CORD

Decide how long you want the finished cord to be and then double this measurement for the length of yarn required. The idea is to hold both ends fairly taut and keep twisting. This job is easier if you have an extra pair of hands to hold the other end. Eventually, if you walk towards each other the cord will twist together on its own. All that remains now is to cut the paper for the pages and the project is complete.

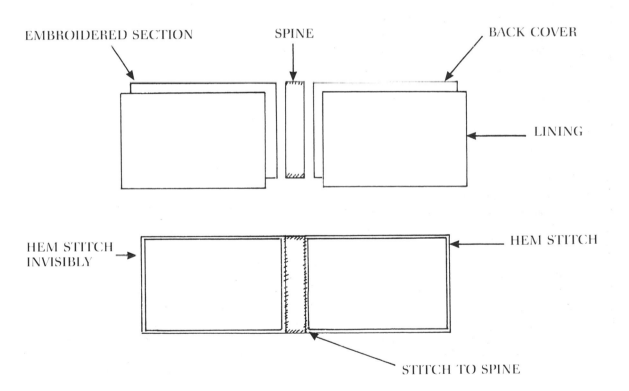

Fig 32 Making up the photograph album

Greek Fishing Village

DARK MINK

WHITE

WHITE RAYON

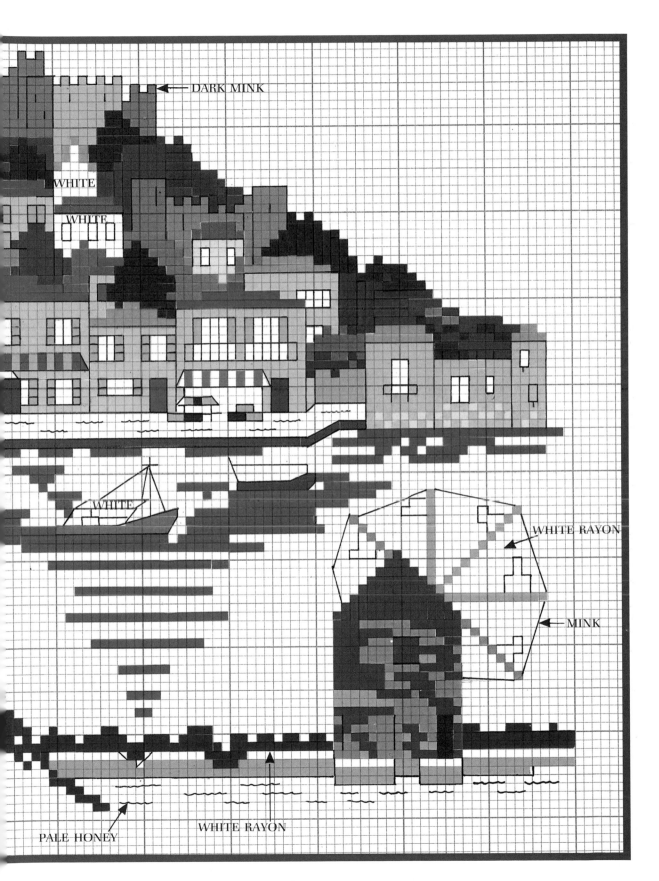

DARK MINK

WHITE

WHITE

WHITE

WHITE RAYON

MINK

PALE HONEY

WHITE RAYON

French House

This rather striking looking house is very simple to stitch. As you will see from the chart, the front of the house is covered in broken plaster, an effect easy to achieve by working patches of the design in similar, but slightly different, shades of stranded cotton blending the areas together.

stitch count: 120×72
design size: 9½×5½in (24×14cm)

MATERIALS

linen in sepia: 26 threads to the inch
stranded cottons as listed on the chart
rayon threads: lime green, scarlet, dark
 red and purple

INSTRUCTIONS

Prepare the linen as described in previous chapters, and work the design from the middle, working towards the edges, following the chart. Stitch the flowers in the window boxes in cross stitch using the rayon threads, and then add the outline, the window frames and the tops of the railings in back stitch.

When complete, press lightly on the wrong side with a warm iron. (Remember that rayon thread will not survive a hot iron.) The design can then be stretched and framed as you like.

Southern US House

stitch count: 99×42
design size: 8×3½in (20×9cm)

MATERIALS

linen in ivory: 25 threads to the inch
strong tea
stranded cottons as listed on the chart

INSTRUCTIONS

The linen for this design was dyed using cold tea. This is an easy way to age linen if you want to attempt to copy an old sampler. All you need to do is make some strong tea and soak the linen overnight and then leave the fabric to dry naturally. This will only work successfully on natural fabrics, as some synthetic mixtures will not dye evenly.

To stitch the house, work from the chart adding the outline as the cross stitch is completed. When the design is finished stretch and mount.

French House

Southern US House

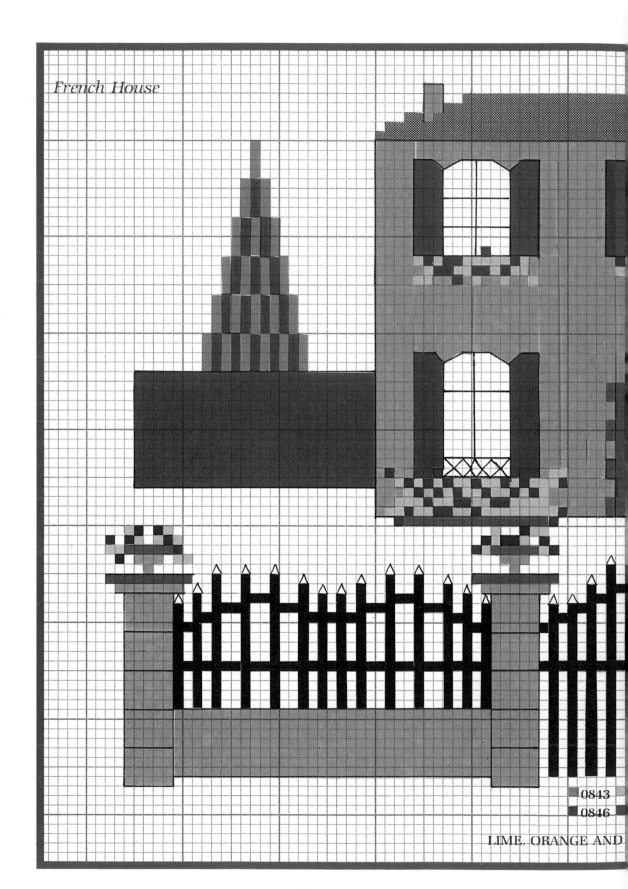

French House

0843
0846

LIME, ORANGE AND

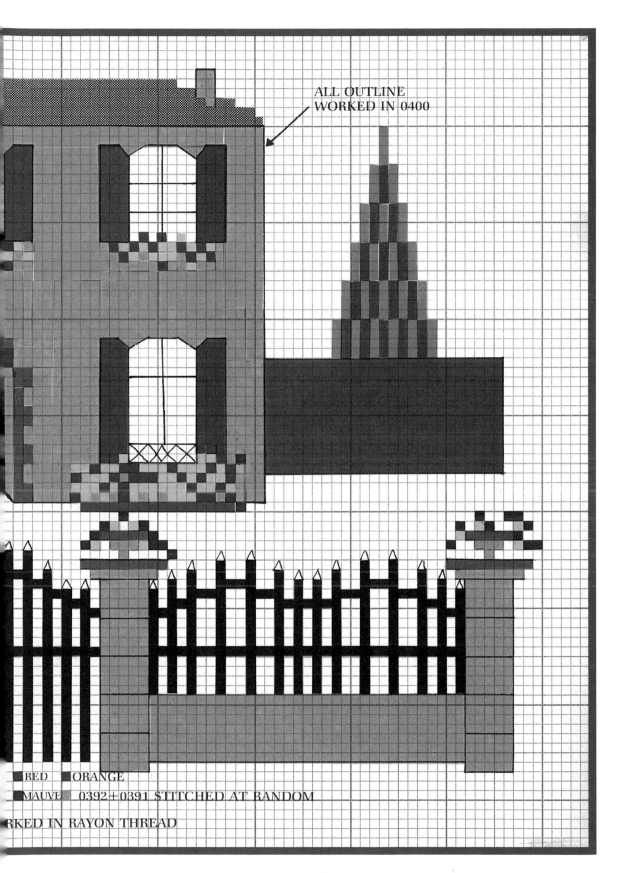

ALL OUTLINE
WORKED IN 0400

RED   ORANGE
MAUVE   0392+0391 STITCHED AT RANDOM
RKED IN RAYON THREAD

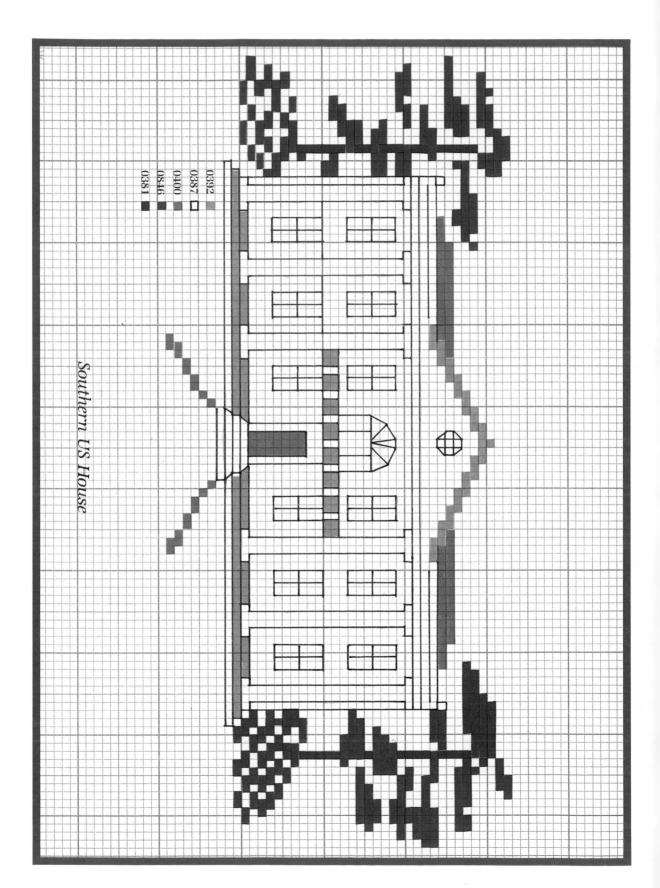

Southern US House

0392
0387
0400
0846
0381

CHAPTER 12
COUNTRY HOUSES IN SILK

These two lovely houses The Oasts and Haystacks are based on real homes (with the kind permission of the owners) and are worked in cross stitch on linen, although both designs would look just as pretty worked on aida fabric or a fine canvas. The theme is one you could extend to any cottage or castle using a feature from the house or garden within the arched border.

WORKING WITH DESIGNER SILKS

Both projects are stitched in Designer Silks which are shaded from the dark to the light end of each shade range (see p 8). This means that the cross stitch will gradually change shade as you stitch without the need to change the shade on the needle each time. It does mean, however, that each cross stitch should be completed individually rather than in two journeys, so that the colours blend gently. All the silk used in this chapter is stitched using one strand only. The charts for both these projects have been designed in sections as the arched borders are symmetrical and the pattern is reversed for the opposite side. As you will see from the evenness of the colour used on the chart, the shaded effect is not indicated here. This will depend entirely on how the design is stitched. Your design will also look different from the worked model in the photograph because you decide where to put the darker or lighter shades whilst stitching.

If you are unable to obtain Designer Silks, any sort of shaded thread would produce a similar effect using the same technique, otherwise stranded cotton could be adapted as follows: group together different shades of one colour (eg greens or brick reds), and put these together on your organiser. When you come to stitch the design pick these shades at random within the colour range on the chart, ie pick from a range of greens for the hops used for the arched border on The Oasts. Thus a shaded effect can be obtained without actually using shaded silk.

The Oasts

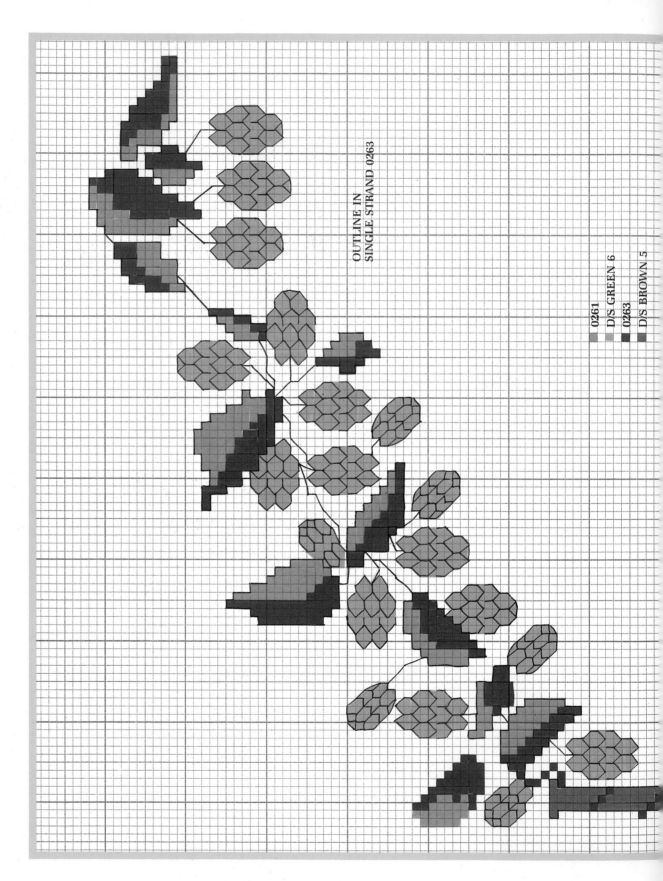

OUTLINE IN
SINGLE STRAND 0263

0261
D/S GREEN 6
0263
D/S BROWN 5

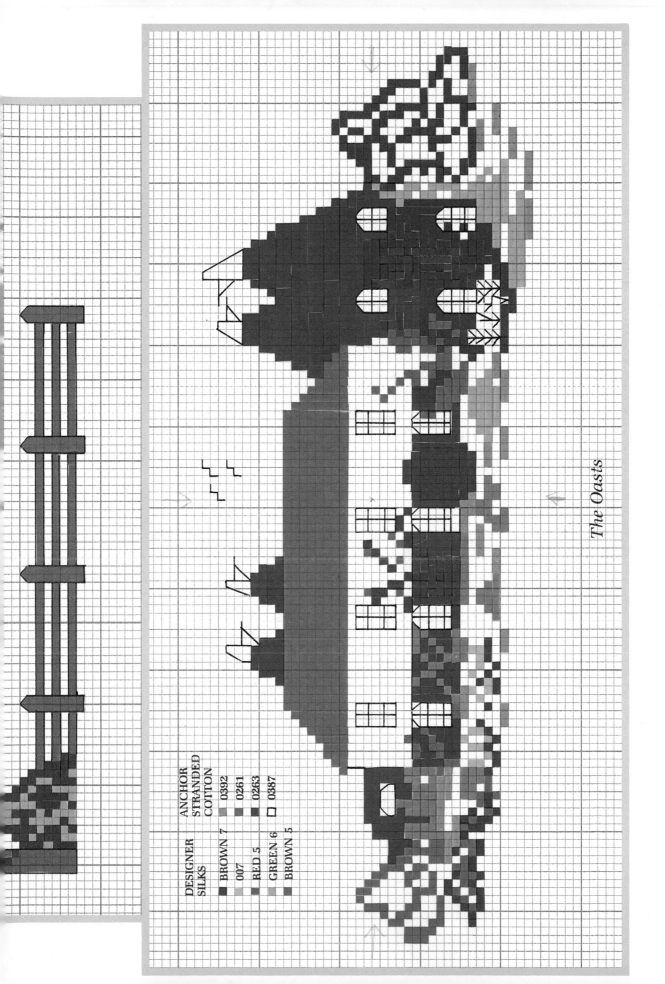

DESIGNER
SILKS

ANCHOR
STRANDED
COTTON

BROWN 7	0392
007	0261
RED 5	0263
GREEN 6	0387
BROWN 5	

The Oasts

The Oasts

This lovely home is owned by the chairman of a well known British company and is a beautifully converted oast house. The front wing of the house is constructed of brick and weather boarding with a tiled roof and includes a magnificent reception room and farmhouse style kitchen. The four oasts have been altered into living accommodation including a marble bathroom, a round study and a bedroom with a tented ceiling – gorgeous!

The gardens are as lovely as the house with a rose and herb garden, a croquet lawn, woodland and an orchard.

The cross stitch design of The Oasts has an arch of hops (the plant from which British beer originates) and a simple picket fence in the foreground.

stitch count: 157×95
design size: 13×8in (33×20cm)

MATERIALS

linen in ivory: 25 threads to the inch
Designer Silks as listed on the chart
stranded cottons as listed on the chart

INSTRUCTIONS

Prepare the linen for sewing as described in earlier chapters (see p 15), marking the centre lines as usual. Begin the design by stitching the house from the chart working from the centre and building up the picture as you sew.

To place the arch, work the central hop (see colour photograph) by placing the bottom two cross stitches either side of the vertical tacking thread, leaving a gap of 25 stitches for the sky above the house. Work each hop as seen on the chart, adding half cross stitches where necessary before working the fine outline in back stitch in a single strand of dark green stranded cotton.

The hop poles are stitched in silk thread, as is the fence in the foreground, but the latter is sewn using just the dark end of the silk thread to give a more definite outline.

The outline on the house is added after the cross stitch is complete using a single strand of dark grey cotton as are the birds above the house. When you are happy with your version of The Oasts, lightly press with a warm iron and stretch and mount as directed in Chapter 15.

Haystacks

This pretty cottage was completely derelict when the present owners bought it seven years ago and lovingly restored it to make a family home. The house is of timber construction with 'wattle and daub' filling the gaps. This means that the original builders, after constructing the timber frame, filled the large areas with small cut sticks which were then covered with a daub of mud (and even animal droppings) to seal the gaps. It was only later that the house would have received a coat of whitewash to improve its appearance. The thatched roof was completely replaced when the house was restored and is covered in wisteria, ivy and old fashioned roses.

The design in the photograph was worked on linen in Designer Silks with small glass beads added to the small vegetable patch in the foreground.

stitch count: 164×95
design size: 12×7in (30×18cm)

MATERIALS

linen in ivory: 25 threads to the inch
Designer Silks as listed on the chart
stranded cottons as listed on the chart
small glass beads: pale green and brown

INSTRUCTIONS

Prepare the fabric as for The Oasts and begin the design by centring the house and working from the middle as before. When the cross stitch is complete, add the outline in one strand of stranded cotton in back stitch. The formal part of the garden is contained within small box hedges, and in the picture has small glass beads added by working a half cross stitch through the hole in the bead and securing each bead as you work.

The remainder of the garden is worked at random building up the colour as you stitch. To place the trees, work out towards them from the linked fence at either side of the house. From this point it should be possible to stitch the wall in the foreground and add the small wrought iron gate using a single strand of black stranded cotton. To complete the design add the arched border starting at either end using stranded cotton for both the cross stitch and the back stitch detail. When the picture is finished, stretch and mount as for The Oasts.

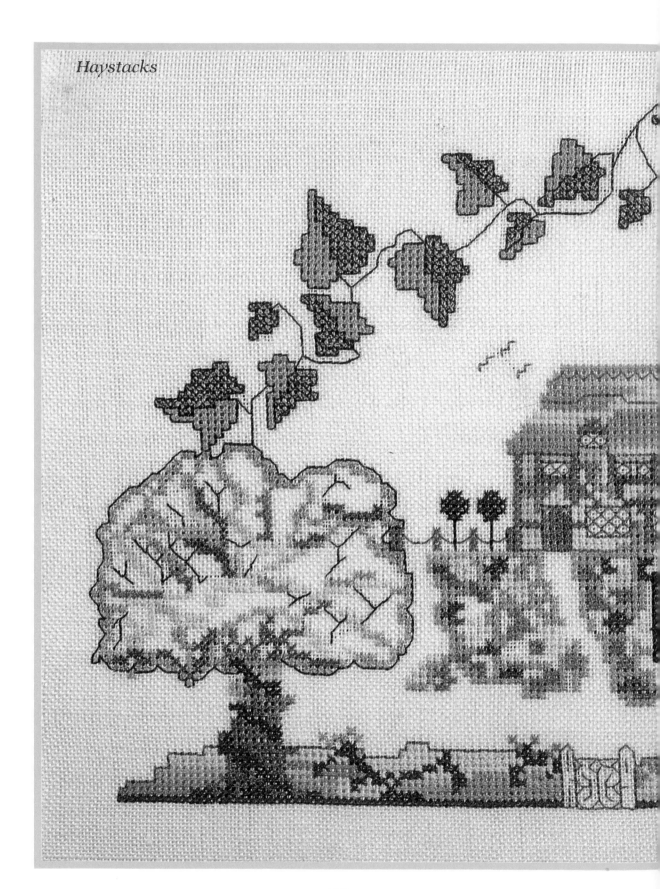

Haystacks

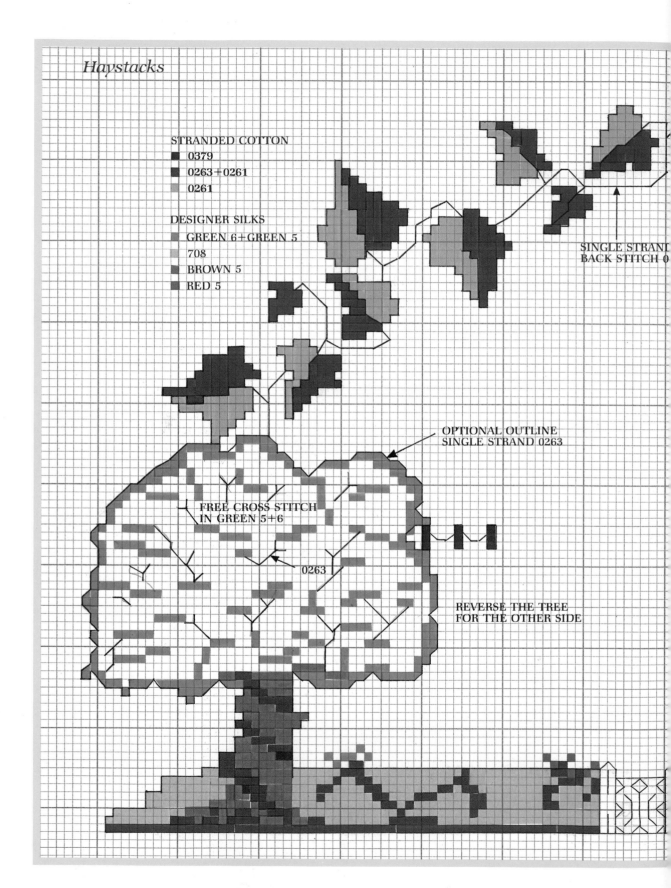

Haystacks

STRANDED COTTON
- 0379
- 0263+0261
- 0261

DESIGNER SILKS
- GREEN 6+GREEN 5
- 708
- BROWN 5
- RED 5

SINGLE STRAN[D]
BACK STITCH 0[...]

OPTIONAL OUTLINE
SINGLE STRAND 0263

FREE CROSS STITCH
IN GREEN 5+6

0263

REVERSE THE TREE
FOR THE OTHER SIDE

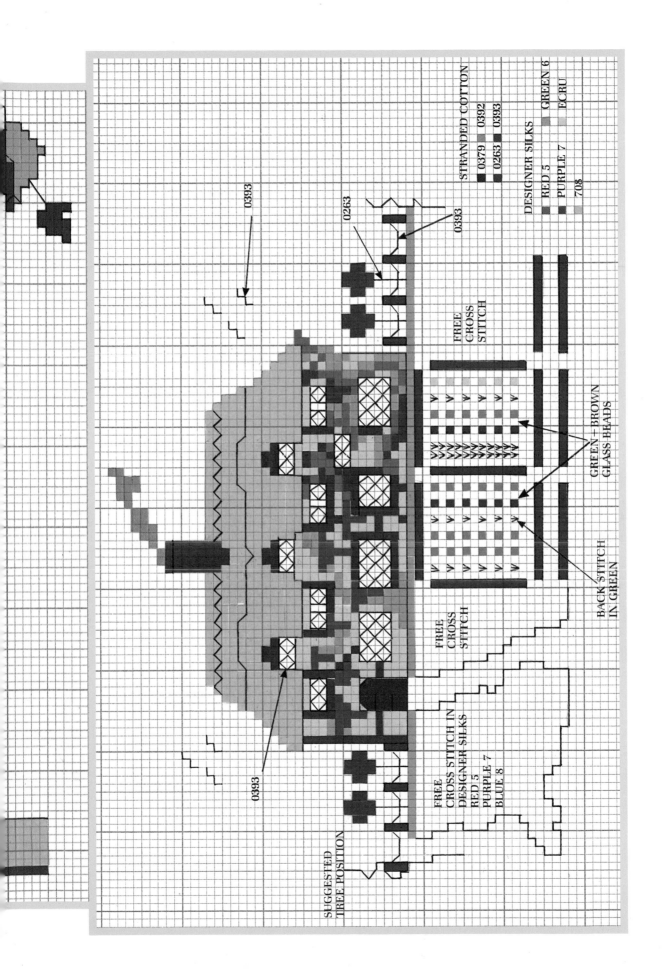

CHAPTER 13
MINIATURE DESIGNS

This simple but charming Rose Cottage has been worked on two media to demonstrate how easy it is to adapt a needlework chart to suit a particular purpose. The scissors case in the photograph is worked on aida using stranded cottons. The miniature version is stitched on silk gauze with one strand of stranded cotton and set in a purpose-made trinket box. The silk gauze is mounted over a small piece of hand-painted silk fabric to add to the design.

Any of the little houses charted in this book could be stitched using these techniques, as long as you check the stitch count to make sure the design will fit.

Rose Cottage Miniature

Evenweave silk gauze is a fine delicate fabric especially produced for the needlework enthusiast and is delightful to work on, although it is very expensive. The silk gauze used in the trinket box actually enables you to work 40 stitches to the inch. The stitches are worked over just one strand of the fabric with each cross completed individually rather than in two journeys.

WORKING ON SILK GAUZE

Before attempting a design using silk gauze, the fabric needs to be prepared in a different way from to that of linen or aida. Silk gauze can be damaged by handling while you stitch from the pressure of your fingers on the fabric, and this is difficult to remove afterwards.

The ideal way to prevent this happening is to prepare the silk fabric as follows.

You will need two small mount boards (like the mount used for framing a picture) and a roll of masking tape.

Cut a piece of silk gauze large enough to allow for framing. Lay one of the mount boards on a clean flat surface and lay the fabric on top, over the opening in the mount (see Fig 33). Carefully stick the gauze in position using the masking tape, cover with the other mount and seal the edges with the tape. The embroidery is worked through the window in the mount.

stitch count: 68×42 (including fence and greenery)
design size: 1¾×1in (4.5×2.5cm)

MATERIALS

silk gauze: 40 stitches to the inch
stranded cottons as listed on the chart
a small piece of silk fabric for the background
silk paints and fixative
a trinket box (optional)

INSTRUCTIONS

Prepare the fabric as described above and carefully count to the centre, placing the first stitch in position as indi-

cated on the colour chart. Build up the picture from the middle completing each cross as you work. For this version, the windows are filled in with cross stitches rather than using the back stitch as in the scissors case. When the picture is finished, carefully remove the design from the homemade frame and set aside.

The silk background is very simple to do, as only a hint of colour is needed. Using a clean brush, mix a little paint to achieve a pale blue and a soft green shade and wash this over the fabric allowing the colour to blend on the horizon. Leave the fabric to dry and then fix the material following the instructions on the bottle (see also instructions for painting silk on p 35). When the fabric is dry, gently wash in warm soapy water and allow to dry naturally.

MAKING UP

Using a warm iron, gently press the needlework on the wrong side and iron the painted fabric to remove all the creases. If using a purchased trinket box, like the one illustrated in the photograph, use the lid as a pattern and

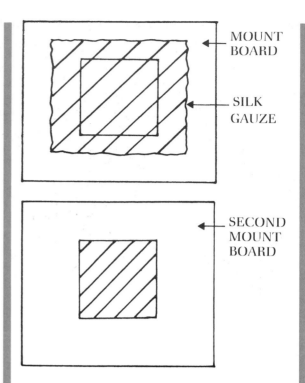

Fig 33 Supporting the silk gauze ready for stitching

carefully cut the gauze and the backing fabric to fit. Make up the miniature as instructed by the manufacturers.

Scissors Case

This project has been stitched on aida using stranded cotton and is self lined, with a small tab to hold the scissors. A few gold needles could be slipped into the lid to make a lovely present for any needle-work enthusiast.

stitch count: 40×28 (the cottage only)
design size: this will depend on the size of the scissors

MATERIALS

aida in cream: 18 blocks to the inch
stranded cottons as listed on the chart
  (use one strand for the cross stitch)
lightweight interfacing
a small piece of lace

INSTRUCTIONS

To estimate the amount of fabric you will need, measure your scissors and allow an inch more in each direction. This becomes the design size which will be doubled for the back section. Allow a little extra for the turnings, and hem the edge to prevent fraying.

Stitch the cottage on the front section and, when complete, press lightly on the wrong side. Cut a piece of interfacing and a piece of aida for the lining. Tack the interfacing to the wrong side of the needlework, turn in the raw edges and stitch the lining in position, edge to edge, using small hem stitches.

To make the tab for the scissors, cut a

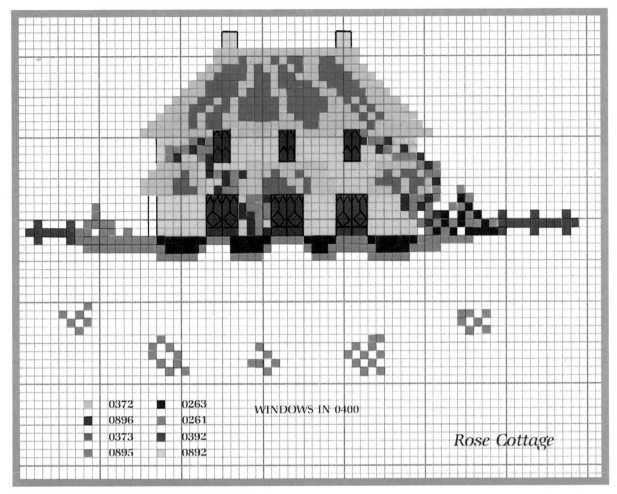

0372 0263
0896 0261 WINDOWS IN 0400
0373 0392
0895 0892

Rose Cottage

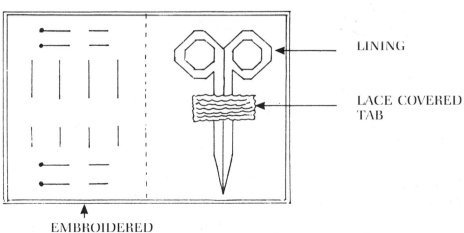

EMBROIDERED
SECTION

Fig 34 Inside view of the scissors case

LINING

LACE COVERED
TAB

piece of aida about 1½in wide, fold in the raw edges and hem invisibly. Carefully stitch the tab in position making sure the scissors will actually fit. A small piece of lace can be stitched over the tab to make it even prettier (see Fig 34).

CHAPTER 14
THREE-DIMENSIONAL COTTAGES

For those who like something a little different, here are two charming cottages in three dimensions. Both designs are worked in half cross stitch (tent stitch), but on different types of canvas.

Little Grey House

This project has been worked on a plastic canvas using tapestry wool. The roof is hinged and has been worked in long stitch with a row of buttonhole stitches around the edge. The whole project has been lined and has a fixed base. It could be used as a safe place to keep string and scissors.

stitch count: 78×31
design size: 7½×3¼in (19×8cm)

MATERIALS

plastic canvas
Appleton Tapestry wools as listed on the chart
thin card (the type from cereal packets is ideal)
lining fabric

INSTRUCTIONS

Cut the four pieces of plastic canvas with a sharp pair of scissors, following a line of squares. If you cut them slightly larger than the design indicates, the material can be trimmed later. To estimate how much canvas you will need, check the stitch count above and count the squares in the canvas. It is that simple. As you will see from the chart, the front and the back of the design are rectangles and the sides are cut to a point. If you feel a little nervous about this, cut the points after you have worked the sides.

The best way to start this project is to sew the stitches for the beams and then the detail can be filled in. All the stitches on the house are worked in half cross stitches (see Fig 27) in the same way as on any single canvas.

Work all four sides from the charts and do not worry about the line down the sides as this will be used to join the pieces together. If you have ever made a gingerbread house the principle is just the same.

Using the same coloured wool as for the beams, line up the four pieces (which should match) and join, stitch for stitch, covering the canvas as you work. You should now have four sides of a box with no top or bottom.

Stand the 'box' on another piece of plastic canvas and cut out a base section. Cover this with half cross stitches in a suitable green and add a simple path to the front door if you wish. Work a row of buttonhole stitch around the edge (see Fig 35) and set aside.

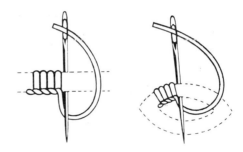

Fig 35 Buttonhole stitch

Standing the house shape on a flat surface, take a large piece of plastic canvas, and, after bending in half (to form the top of the roof), stand it on top of your house to cut the roof shape. Remember to allow for the overhang. When you are satisfied that the roof is the right size, work a row of buttonhole stitches around the edge to cover the canvas. Now you need to fill in the rest.

Work one row of continuous long stitch along the brow of the roof, and then count to the centre. Work four long stitches, two either side of the centre and work out towards the border (see Fig 36). The idea is to work the long stitches in blocks of four and stagger the blocks to end up with a type of brick effect. As you near the edge, continue the pattern right up to the stitched border. Then put it all together.

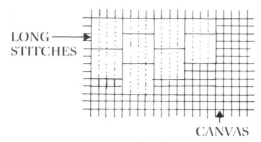

LONG→
STITCHES

CANVAS

Fig 36 Long stitch

MAKING UP

To line the house, cut pieces of thin card slightly smaller than the four sides of the house. Using the card as a pattern, cut some lining fabric allowing enough fabric for turnings.

The lining will be laced over the card, which can then be stitched inside the house. It not only covers the back of the work, but the card lining also helps the house to keep its shape. Follow the same procedure for the roof and the base.

Join the roof to the house starting at the centre and working out to the sides including the gable at the end. If you want the lid to open, leave the front unstitched.

Join the house to the base using green yarn. To make the grass around the house so that it will neatly cover the join, use a stabbing motion, up and down but leave a loop on the right side. Where the house has flowers growing up the side, add some of the same shade amongst the grass.

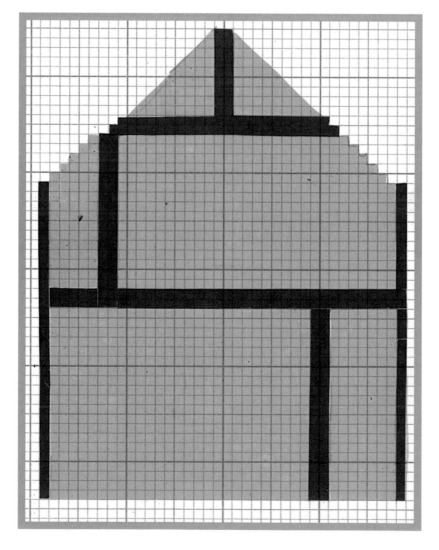

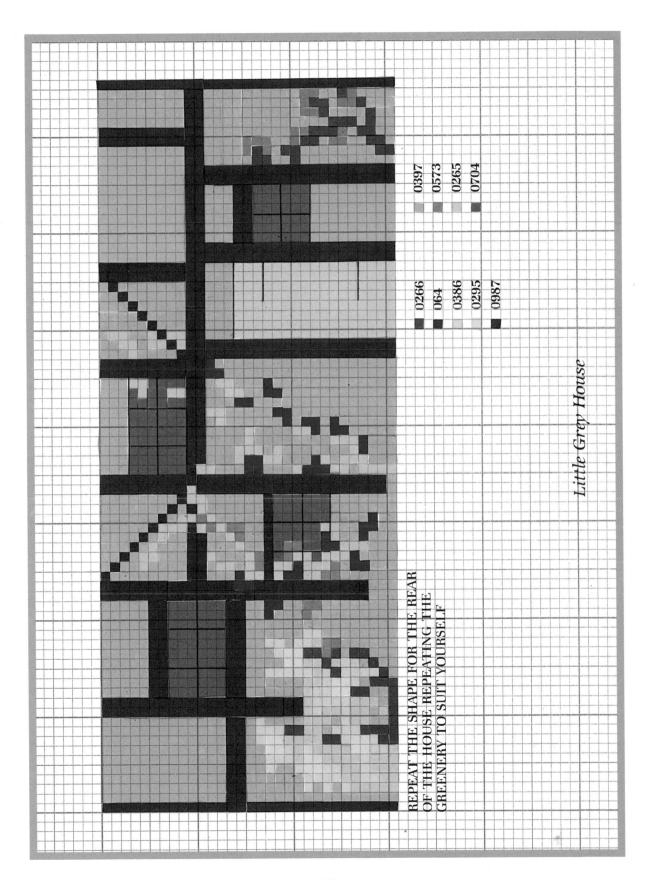

REPEAT THE SHAPE FOR THE REAR
OF THE HOUSE REPEATING THE
GREENERY TO SUIT YOURSELF

0266
064
0386
0295
0987

0397
0573
0265
0704

Little Grey House

Peach Tree House

This design has been made into a door-stop and is actually a covered house brick. The main design is on the top with a repeating pattern of trees and a picket fence worked around the sides. The cottage on the top could be used for any of the cross stitch projects in the book, as could the simple tree designs. The size of this project will depend on the size of your house brick. For this reason, there is no stitch count or design size quoted for the model in the photograph. The design can be extended to fit your brick or whatever you want to put in it.

MATERIALS

single canvas in white: 14 stitches to the inch
Appleton crewel wool as listed on the chart
lightweight polyester wadding

INSTRUCTIONS

To estimate the canvas requirements, measure your brick. Carefully measure the length, width and depth of the brick and write down these dimensions. Now look at the diagram, Fig 37, to see the shape of the canvas. You will need to allow extra canvas for the top section as the stitches will contract the canvas slightly, so increase this dimension a little. As you will see from the diagram, the side seams are slashed diagonally before making up, but leave the canvas un-cut until the needlework is finished.

Cut out a large rectangle and allow for the canvas to be laced under the brick. Using the measurements taken from the brick and a soft pencil, draw the shape on the canvas as described in Fig 37. The arrows marked on the diagram show in which direction to stitch.

To stitch the design, mark the top section with centre lines and work the cottage from the chart in half cross stitch (see Fig 27), using three strands of crewel wool. As with any other charted design, work the cottage from the middle and out towards the border. Leave stitching the background canvas until the end. Count and position the fence and the trees on the side sections and stitch these following the chart. When the design is finished, stitch the background as indicated on the chart.

MAKING UP THE HOUSE BRICK

Lightly press the needlework on the wrong side with a damp cloth, block out the canvas as described on p 116 and leave to dry. Cut diagonal slashes as described in the diagram, fold the excess fabric inside and join the material, edge to edge, matching the stitches and using matching yarn. Trim away the excess fabric and press lightly on the wrong side.

Wrap the brick carefully in the polyester wadding and stitch this in position. Now gently slip the canvas over the brick and lace the excess canvas across the bottom. To prevent the base of the brick scratching any surfaces cut a piece of felt and stitch to the bottom.

Fig 37 The shape of the house brick canvas

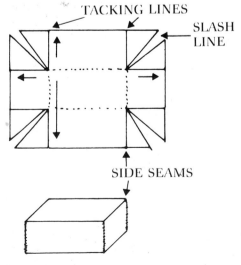

Fig 38 Making up the house brick

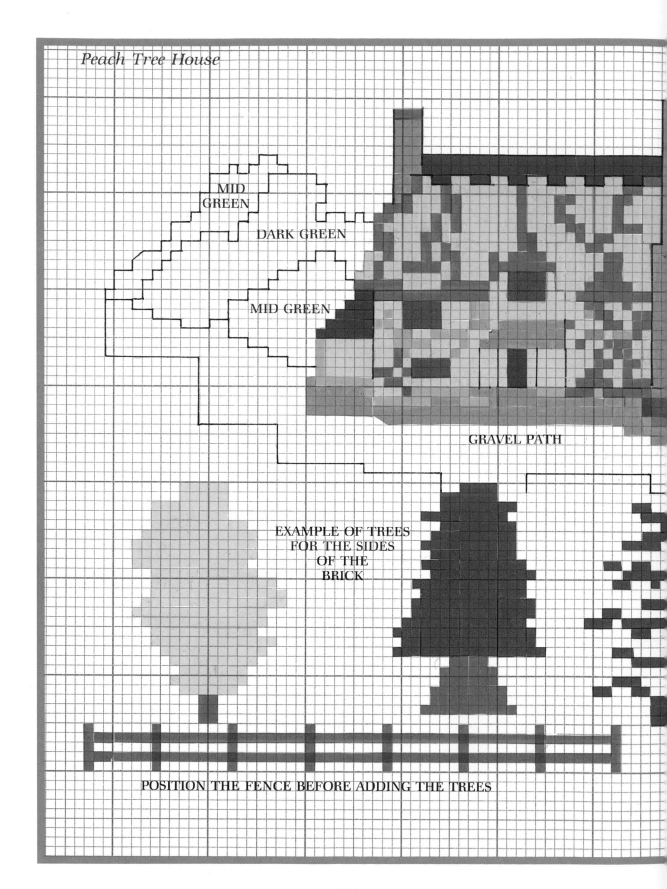

Peach Tree House

MID GREEN

DARK GREEN

MID GREEN

GRAVEL PATH

EXAMPLE OF TREES
FOR THE SIDES
OF THE
BRICK

POSITION THE FENCE BEFORE ADDING THE TREES

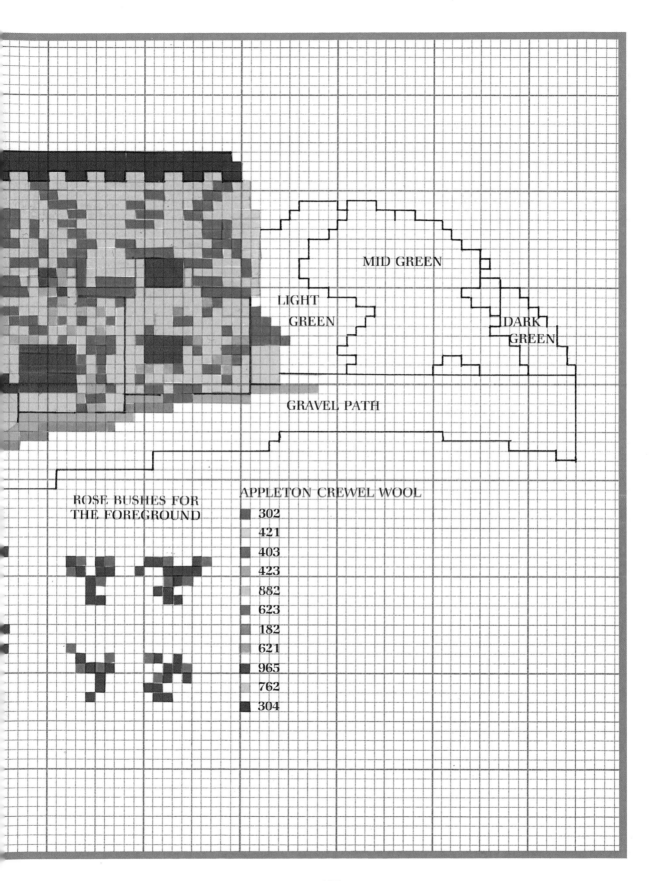

MID GREEN

LIGHT
GREEN

DARK
GREEN

GRAVEL PATH

ROSE BUSHES FOR
THE FOREGROUND

APPLETON CREWEL WOOL

302
421
403
423
882
623
182
621
965
762
304

CHAPTER 15
FINISHING TOUCHES

There are a few important rules to adhere to when stretching and framing a piece of needlework to prevent spoiling all your hard work. Ignorance of the management of textiles during the mounting and stretching process has probably caused the demise of many priceless pieces of needlework.

These basic guidelines will ensure success.

1 Always use acid-free paper or card (available from good stationery or art shops) to prevent damage to the fabric.
2 Use natural threads, ie cotton or linen, for any extra stitching.
3 If you have to use an adhesive make it rubber based.
4 Do not overstretch the needlework, but cut the mount board to exactly the right size.
5 Always have sufficient space between the glass and the needlework so that the embroidery is not in contact with the glass.

Mounting Needlework

To make up your design as a picture it is worth the time and effort to mount the piece yourself rather than sending the work to a framer in its raw state. It will be much cheaper and really doesn't take long once you have mastered the technique.

Either use acid-free mount card or cover other card with acid-free paper. It is also possible to cover a piece of card with a natural fabric (cotton ideally) which can be fixed with a rubber-based adhesive and left to dry. Canvas pieces will need slightly different management before mounting, and this will be covered separately.

There are two basic methods of attaching the piece to the mount board:
1 Pin the work to the edge of the board and stitch in place (see Fig 40).
2 Pin the work to the board and lace across the back using strong linen thread (see Fig 41).

When pinning a piece of linen or aida to the edge of your covered mount board it must be centred and stretched evenly, ensuring that all the margins are the same. (It is customary to leave a slightly larger border at the bottom of a picture.) Once the board is cut to size and prepared for mounting, measure across the bottom edge and mark the centre with a glass headed pin. Take the worked piece of needlework and mark the centre stitch along the bottom with a pin and match these up to ensure that the fabric is on in the right place. Working out from the centre of each edge, pin through the fabric following a line of threads until all four sides are complete.

If using method 1, stitch through the needlework and the fabric covering the board using strong thread (natural origin) and removing the pins as you go (see Fig 40).

For method 2, the spare fabric is laced across the back of the board, two sides at a time (see Fig 41).

Whichever method you prefer, always work on clean surfaces and with clean hands. This is particularly important in hot weather when your hands perspire. Make sure the base plate of the iron is spotlessly clean, as ironed-on marks can be very difficult to remove.

Fig 39 Pinning the fabric to a mount board

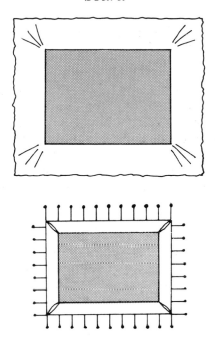

Fig 40 Stitching to a mount board

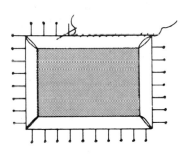

Fig 41 Lacing over a mount board

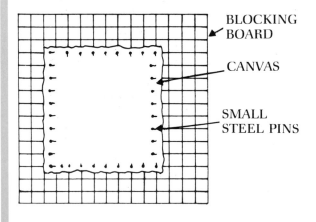

Mounting Canvas

Canvas may need more stretching than linen or aida as it is often covered in stitches and may be more distorted as a result. Purpose-made boards are available for blocking out – with lines to check the right angles at the corners – although a set square would suffice.

Using rust-free thumb tacks, pin the canvas to the board, following the lines on the board, dampening slightly if necessary. When the whole canvas is pinned all the way round, leave to dry before mounting as described above.

BLOCKING BOARD

CANVAS

SMALL STEEL PINS

Fig 42 Blocking out a canvas

ACKNOWLEDGEMENTS

I would like to thank the following people for the help and support I have received whilst writing this book.

Michel Standley, for organising me and the stitching;

Isabel Elliott, Stanley Duller, Heather Cook, Jo Verso, Susie Dodds and Karin Walton.

The enthusiastic stitchers without whom all would have been lost: Hanne Castelo, Dorothy Presley, Ruth Mowat, Elizabeth Smith and Vera Greenoff.

Jean and Frank Dittrich of Pot Pourri etc, Los Angeles, USA for ideas, enthusiasm and hospitality.

The Earl and Countess St Aldwyns, Glos, for permission to use their property and their village for inspiration.

Pat and Eric Fowler for their unique contribution.

Sarah Shaw for constant help and support.

I would also like to thank the following companies for the supplies used in the book:

The Graphic Centre, Cheltenham.

The Campden Needlecraft Centre, Chipping Campden.

Tunley's of Swindon.

The Ladies Work Society, Moreton in the Marsh.

Framecraft Miniatures Ltd, Birmingham.

Simon Deighton, Newton Abbot.

Lucy Coltman of Designer Silks, Hook Norton, Oxfordshire.

The Irish Linen Depot, Ealing, London.

BIBLIOGRAPHY

Fifty Counted Thread Embroidery Stitches (Coats Publication, 1982)

Cook, Olive *English Cottages and Farmhouses* (Thames and Hudson, 1982)

Johnstone, Pauline *Three Hundred Years of Embroidery 1600–1900* (Wakefield Press, 1986)

King, Donald *Samplers: Victoria and Albert Museum* (HMSO, 1960)

Lewis, Felicity *Needlepoint Samplers* (Cassell, 1981)

Mundle, Liz & Eaton, Jan *The Cross Stitch and Sampler Book* (Methuen, 1985)

Sebba, Anne *Samplers, The Gentle Craft* (Weidenfeld & Nicholson, 1979)

Verso, Jo *Picture in Cross Stitch* (David & Charles, 1988)

Warren, Verina *Landscape in Embroidery* (Batsford 1986)

INDEX